Actor Nicholas Pennell:
Risking Enchantment

Mary Z. Maher

GW00507754

PublishAmerica
Baltimore

First printing

ISBN: 1-4137-3808-7
'LISHED BY PUBLISHAMERICA, LLLP
www.publishamerica.com
Baltimore

'd in the United States of America

Acknowledgments-

I WOULD LIKE TO THANK the Canadian Studies Research Program at the Canadian Embassy in Washington, D.C. for a grant to research this book. Thanks also to the Fondazione Bogliosco, at the Centro Study Ligure in Italy, for a residency which provided time away from my job, a quiet place to work, and the stimulation of other artists, a context conducive to writing this book.

I reserve my special gratitude for the Stratford Festival itself, whose Archivists Lisa Brandt and Janie Edmonds patiently provided information as well as moral support throughout the project. These two people gave unstintingly of their time and their considerable analytical skills throughout my research and on into the production process. Roy Brown was a pillar of strength and a master of detail, the ideal advisor for a project such as this one. Ron Nichol gave influential opinions while Michael Halberstam offered encouragement. All of the artists included contributed lavishly of their personal time, especially Richard Monette, now Artistic Director of the Festival, Pat Galloway, John Broome, Janet Wright, Marti Maraden, Stephen Ouimette, and Nicholas Rudall.

Other people have supported me throughout with painstaking editing work and copy suggestions: Professor Margaret Knapp and Judy Maher. My computer support person, Chris Zwemke, was of immeasurable help. My special publishing advisor, Jura Sherwood, needs to be commended for patiently listening.

The photograph on the cover of Nicholas Pennell and his faithful dog Pook is through the good graces of Frank Holte, who took it in Stratford. The family photos were given to me by Robin and Jenny Pennell, who not only provided essential narrative but gave generously of their time to welcome me to Devon. The professional photos were courtesy of the Stratford Festival in Stratford, Ontario, Canada. My colleagues there helped to make it a home away from home for me during several summers of researching the biography.

The book, of course, is dedicated to Nicholas Pennell.

Table of Contents

I.
Prologue

NICHOLAS PENNELL GRANTED ME INTERVIEW TIME in August of 1994, in Stratford, Ontario, Canada, when he was performing in three plays at the Stratford Festival and also playing the lead in a CBC television production. Midway through our summer conversations, Pennell's voice trembled and he suddenly said, "I just—I can't emphasize enough the joy the work gives me. It really does give me a great deal of pleasure. I'm not an actor who feels miserable all the time." His interjection into our discussion was weighty and unusual, but I did not yet understand why.

Six months later, he was dead of lymphatic cancer at the age of 56. I read that his favorite lines from Shakespeare were among Hamlet's last words: "If thou didst ever hold me in thy heart, / Absent thee from felicity a while, / And in this harsh world draw thy breath in pain, / To tell my story." Later on in 1995 after his death, I started to research this biography, and then I did indeed draw my breath in pain as I began.

Nicholas Pennell's acting career was remarkable. English by birth, his life as a performer began in 1958, alongside a group of John Osborne's angry young actors at the Royal Academy of Dramatic Art and continued with acting onstage and on television in London, most notably in the hallmark role of Michael Mont in *The Forsyte Saga*.

After he moved to Canada in 1972, he played over 77 parts with the Stratford Festival. His work included the great Shakespearean title roles in *Hamlet, Pericles, Richard II, Richard III, Macbeth, King John,* and *Titus Andronicus* as well as Ariel and Stephano in *Tempest,* the Fool in *King Lear,* Malvolio in *Twelfth Night,* Iago in *Othello,* Jacques in *As You Like It,* Oberon in *A Midsummer Night's Dream,* and Ulysses in *Troilus and Cressida.* He gave definitive performances of Thomas Becket in *Murder in the Cathedral,* Victor in *Private Lives,* Jack in *Home,* and Jack Worthing in *The Importance of Being Earnest.* He created the role of Leonard Woolf in *Virginia,* in tandem with Maggie Smith playing the lead character, a production which transferred to the Haymarket in London, and he worked with Robertson Davies in the adaptation of the novel *World of Wonders,* bringing the character of Magnus Eisengrim to the stage. He toured as Siegfried Sassoon in *Not About Heroes* and performed it in Chicago along with *Pygmalion*'s Henry Higgins. A recipient of the Tyrone Guthrie Award and a nominee for the Joseph Jefferson Award, Pennell accumulated over 250 television credits on BBC and CBC and was in six films, including *Isadora* and *The Battle of Britain.*

Over the course of time it has taken to write this book, people have asked me, "Why this actor?" The question comes only from those who had never seen Nicholas Pennell onstage. First of all, Nicky had charisma, which is something an actor has or hasn't. He was natural and comfortable on a stage and his presence captivated people. Secondly, he had a sagacity and discernment that was unmistakable and to which others were drawn. One had the feeling Nicky had much more to say once he was away from the crowd. He was prudently articulate and boundlessly witty. He relished talking about acting. Once an actor challenged me during an interview, saying, "Why should I give you my secrets!"— Nicky gave away his secrets hourly. He lived to plumb the mysteries of performance, to elucidate, to explicate, never to confound, only to expound.

Secondly, he began a flourishing career in England and then made a decisive turn into Canada and a final settlement with a resident classical company, where he remained an actor. No detours, no second thoughts. Acting was clearly a calling, a vocation.

In 1992, I published my first book, *Modern Hamlets and Their Soliloquies*, a scholarly text that received critical recognition and was moderately successful commercially. I'd begun collecting interviews for a second book, this one focusing on how experienced classical actors prepared to play Shakespearean roles. I gathered data from English speaking actors—at that time, Tony Church, Judi Dench, Derek Jacobi, Kevin Kline, and Zoe Caldwell had been interviewed. However, I was familiar with the Stratford Festival and clearly it offered the best Shakespeare in North America, with a very high standard of acting and production values. Naturally, I wanted Canadian actors well-represented in my second book.

I had the most in common with Nicholas Pennell. He was a man who was literate and literary. He talked about *text* all the time: It was the center of his philosophy and the continuing raw material of his performances. He often taught (during the off-seasons) at the University of Michigan, where I'd gotten my Ph.D. 30 years ago in the esoteric field of oral interpretation. As a graduate student, I used to travel to Stratford to see the work of Pennell and his colleagues. Nicky—as his friends called him and as I soon began to think of him in my head—had played in all but one of Shakespeare's plays. He had performed one-man readings of poetry and prose, and he qualified as a singer of tales. Our lives inter-stitched, enmeshed. We were destined to have some lively conversations.

I depend a great deal on the interview process, which in turn invests faith in the actor's facility of *memoriae*. Experience has proven that, just like the Shakespearean schoolboys who were given the assignment of memorizing Sunday's sermon (as it was being spoken) in order to write it in class on Monday, this proficiency in remembering—along with "muscle memory," the act of remembering what the body did associated with what the mind told the mouth to say—is extremely well-developed in the classical actor.

One night in the 1980s, I was having dinner with Paul Whitworth, Artistic Director at Shakespeare-Santa Cruz. As we talked about *Love's Labour's Lost*, he surprised himself by quoting huge passages of the play he had performed with the Royal Shakespeare Company in the 1970s. Astonishingly, he quoted other people's parts, parts he had never played. When I interviewed Ben Kingsley fourteen years after his Hamlet at The Other Place in Stratford-upon-Avon, he had a perfect sensory memory of the stage space, could even smell the room, and then proceeded to draw his entrances and exits for that performance on paper. Judi Dench once said to me, "Name any act or scene in *A Midsummer Night's Dream*. I can quote it all. The whole play. Also *Twelfth Night*. Any role, any line. They're all up here" (she tapped her head).

Memory is one of the actor's chief tools: It is the instrument behind learning lines and in calling up the choices and materials actualized in rehearsal and in performance. Alas, it is also fallible, impermanent, and capable of being embellished. Memory is nonetheless what we use to construct and re-construct ourselves, who we think we are, who we think we ought to be. Although imperfect, it can recapture mood, *milieu*, and the essentials of performance. When I interview actors, I send the final draft to the interviewee to emend or edit, to make sure that I am hearing what the actor is trying to say and not getting in the way of it or distorting it. This not only keeps me out of court, but it gets closer to what the actor considers to be his or her truth. Sadly, that wasn't possible with Nicholas Pennell.

What was possible was to go to other remembrancers. I

tape-recorded interviews with a number of his friends and colleagues to supplement the research in the Stratford Archives, beginning with actors and colleagues who shared the artistic work with him—Richard Monette, Pat Galloway, Marti Maraden, Stephen Ouimette, Janet Wright, John Broome, Patsy Rodenburg, Carole Shelley, Brian Bedford, Desmond Heeley, Domini Blythe, and Edward Atienza. I spoke with Nicky's brother and sister-in-law in Devonshire, Robin and Jenny Pennell. They introduced me to two other friends from Nicky's youth, Clare Showell and Sebastian Breaks. I had extended conversations with the core of friends that Nicky worked with in Chicago—Nicholas Rudall, Michael Halberstam, and David New, and have corresponded and spoken with a number of others for additional data, including Claribel Baird, Zelma Weisfeld, and Tom Loewe at the University of Michigan. And of course, I have also thoroughly researched his performance life, reading dozens of newspaper and journal articles about him in addition to collecting interview data from associates.

I had considerable help from Roy Brown, who created the properties for productions at the Avon and Tom Patterson theaters, and Lisa Brant, Archivist at the Festival. Roy Brown was executor of Pennell's estate and took Nicky through the final weeks of his incurable illness. Brant had organized one of the best theater archives in the world. She and her accomplished assistant Jane Edmonds (who subsequently became the Archivist) made sure that I had every resource available in writing the book. These three people knew everything there was to know about Nicky's work at the Festival. On my request, Lisa Brant carried out an interview with Marti Maraden. The project became collaborative in a very positive way.

Brant was invaluable in helping to locate an extensive spoken history of Nicholas Pennell. His life was measured out in interviews. Although these varied in scope and weight, there were records of Nicky on radio or on video from 1977 (he first appeared at the Festival in 1972), 1979, 1981, 1982, 1984, 1989 (two mutual admirers, Stratford's education director Pat Quigley and Nicky, make this one a treasure), 1993, and my own interview in 1994, in which Nicky talked with me for six hours over two days.

It is extremely rare for an artist whose work disappears after the curtain call each night to be so thoroughly documented, his ideas and his methods of working recorded and kept. There is another thing about the interviews of Nicholas. He was invited onto radio and onto television because his public wanted to hear a fearless and stimulating talker. Nicky always performed his own text. His whole body of work exemplified the pronouncing, the discoursing he had done about being a working actor. Just as he preached about performing Shakespeare: Those plays were not meant to be analyzed and agonized over—they were meant to be acted. There was work to be done. Get on with it.

One writer described Nicky's interview style:

> While actors generically are given to histrionic interviews, Nicholas Pennell often speaks as cautiously as a politician, qualifying his statements in lines of subjunctive clauses, and frequently punctuating his observations with an earnest "Do you understand what I mean?" He replies to the interviewer's every question with long paragraphs of carefully constructed prose, which spill from the tape recorder to the page as though edited for publication. He chooses each word and phrase deliberately, and pauses long and often with a contemplative air which discourages interruption as he arranges his next thesis. Anger he expresses with the diction of one with fifteen years' acting experience, rendering petty the clumsy expressions of us amateurs....[1]

You can hear this caution with words in Nicky's voice on the interview tapes (although he would surely regret being compared to a politician). I would call his spoken discourse *lawyerly* except that he was more concerned with articulating the truth than with persuading his listeners. As a young actor he spoke very quickly, in a near-tenor voice which grabbed the lapels of the interviewer. As he grew older, the voice deepened to a baritone and sounded way off into the future distance. The sentences were heavy with qualifiers and included an occasional gulp of air that carried him over several long phrases.

Although Nicky's life had loss and disappointment as well as fulfillment and triumph, his personal metaphor was "giving a performance." Not characterizing it or intuiting it, although that was involved, but giving it. He was an artist whose *oeuvre* was situated in a unique setting, a theater company of working actors much like Shakespeare's. His beneficiaries were audiences, students, friends, and the curious. He was positive and generous and filled with the inclination to share. First and foremost a fine actor, he also strewed life-changing gifts, a godfather no one could stop.

One evening, he was listening on the car radio to poets being interviewed on "CBC Arts Tonight":

> I was driving home from having been up to the lake all afternoon and I thought to myself, Now why, every time when you hear a poet or a novelist do you hear about the memoirs they are writing. I thought, what are memoirs? What are they about? They are autobiographical but they are not actually the book about your life. They're a series of reflections on your life. I think acting is a memoir in a funny kind of way, it's a form of reflecting on one's life. Does that make sense?[2]

I hope that it does, because it is what I must do here. Nicky would never have written his memoirs, hardly wrote letters, was a teller and not a recorder. He conducted his life out of large boxes. He would receive correspondence, a bill, a contract, an old lease, a postcard from Maggie Smith, a message about the water purifier, fan mail—and he tossed all of it into a box. He threw nothing away nor prioritized one piece of mail over another. Near the end of his life, as word went out about his illness, floods of letters arrived. These, in all their brilliance and effusion and sadness, began to flesh out the actor as a human being and to tell the details of his story.

After sorting through three cartons of his papers, I realized that I did not know what Nicky's handwriting looked like. There was no diary, no daily calendar. Perhaps it was natural that the paper trail was sparse: An actor keeps everything in his head, doesn't he—since he is a master of memory. But not so much as a grocery list?

Near the end of the final interview, Nicky began talking about a performance he (bravely) gave to the Shakespeare Association of America in 1986. He read from the *Variorum Hamlet*, a book which footnotes each line of dialogue and records, with painstaking detail, the quantity of commentary that various editors down through the ages have written about that play. The book has a few lines of dialogue at the top of the page, and the remainder is filled with editors' footnotes about how they interpreted that particular line. This got enormously funny if read solemnly and, "the academics, especially, were rolling on the floor. What they didn't see and what was so funny, was they were looking at themselves in the Big Mirror." Nicky was referring to *Hamlet*, "the mirror up to nature" which every actor mythically holds as he performs, so that his audience can see not only him, in all his humanness, but themselves as well.

This sweet and complicated man was a born raconteur and his own stories got embroidered and took shape as he fictionalized and constructed himself. What was "the truth," beyond the factual data I could unearth? For each of us, and especially for a performer, our truths are time-bound, our truths are memoirs written by someone else, and our truths risk enchantment when we tell them.

I shared my worries with Stephen Ouimette, a colleague of Nicky's: "In telling his story I feel a burden the size of which you must feel when they handed you the script of *Hamlet.*" Ouimette answered, "I have one piece of advice. Don't think ahead to the whole book. Just get through the first beat."[3] Nicky often quoted this passage from T.S. Eliot's *Four Quartets*:

.... There is no competition—
There is only the fight to recover what has been lost
And found and lost again and again: and now, under conditions
That seem unpropitious. But perhaps neither gain nor loss.
For us, there is only the trying. The rest is not our business.

Writing, like acting, is a performance. It is about creating an illusion. It, too, is all smoke and mirrors.

II.
Trivial Fond Records

ONE REMARKABLE FACT about Pennell's childhood was that he grew up during World War II in England. He was born on 19 November 1938 on a farm in Devon that happened to be strategically located:

> In the west country, which people think of as being relatively unscathed...we had lots of evacuees sent to us. We were in "Bomb Alley," the corridor between Plymouth and the Channel and [the Germans] were trying to hit the dockyards.... They used to off-load the bombs on their return, so my godfather would put lanterns out in the field (because inside the houses we had the blackout curtains), and very often they'd bomb the fields where the lanterns were.
>
> Another nice little habit... was... the fighter escorts. I can remember once I was in kindergarten coming home from school and walking up the main street of Brixham with the other children. I must have been about 4, I suppose. I heard this buzzing and the fighter plane came and machine-gunned right up the street. I can remember a woman running out of a shop and throwing me down in the gutter and lying down on top of me.
>
> So we did experience the war.[4]

When Nicky told this story on radio, he said that he could remember hearing the bullets hit the ground. In another interview, it was his mother who threw her body over him.[5] Children who grew up in wartime have anxieties about security. The images in the newspapers and the forms and pressures of the age could not help but imprint those who were remembrancers.

Nicky also mentioned that he was growing up almost entirely in the society of women since most of the men, including his father, were away at war. All the farm work was done by women and he said his mother was an early feminist. In a later interview in *Windsor Review*, he made these statements about his "Thoughts on Childhood":

> We never had an actor in the family.
> My mother was an alcoholic.
> ....
> I liked role playing and dress up.
> My mother made me a brown and yellow elf
>   costume.
> My mother read regularly to me. *Winnie the Pooh*
>   and *Wind in the Willows*.
> My father was away in the war. I do not remember
>   him clearly.
> ....
> My mother influenced me most.
> ....
> When I was ten I became aware of my first
>   perception of beauty—the sea. We lived by the
>   sea. I constantly go back to the comfort of the sea.[6]

A number of the themes in Nicky's life are encapsulated in these remarks. More information about his childhood comes from an interview on a couple of radio programs fashioned after the British "Desert Island Disks" show on BBC, where a celebrity interviewee is stranded in a remote place with no hope of rescue but may select five pieces of music to have on the island. Nicky selected a nostalgic tune called "Underneath the Arches," a post-Depression era song about down-and-outers sleeping under the arches at Charing Cross.[7] He resented being sent to bed in the summer evenings when it was still light outside and would have preferred playing in the garden. He had a clear visual image of the large mahogany wind-up gramophone with its horns as speakers, and his mother selecting records like "The Parting Song" and the wartime tunes of Vera Lynn to play after dinner.

Although there was almost no theater during the war, Nicky was taken to the movie *Bambi*. He cried so much when the mother doe died that he had to be removed from the cinema. One of his early career aspirations was wanting to be an admiral and to serve pink gins to his family in the cabin of his ship.[8] However, there was no exposure to theater beyond the "panto's" or Christmas pantomimes, that rare English holiday entertainment which adds vaudeville and music hall to children's stories. Other than the usual dressing-up and inventing characters that most children do, and the abundance of games children play when pushed to their own imaginative resources, Nicky claimed that there were few distinct things that spoke to him about becoming an actor. This assertion was not borne out by others' stories of his youth.

A first major sense of loss came at about age 7, when he was sent off to boarding school:

> I remember standing on the porch outside Allhallow's (a very big building) and crying and crying and calling to my mother "I won't do it again" as she left, because I thought I'd done something bad. Being at school for nine or ten

months of the year from that age up to [the age of] eighteen years was emotionally a rocky situation—I don't know where I'm going with this—but I think the need to portray an emotional state and a life, to project somebody else's existence, a character on a page, comes from (somewhere along the line) needing to be liked or approved of or loved in some way since I lacked that kind of nurturing in my childhood. That's really cheap psychology, but it's a possibility.

These experiences signal the beginnings of the histrionic imagination, the constructing of one's past as an emotionally vulnerable person, a sensory being who remembers the sharpness of feelings from earlier years and places oneself at the center of heroic narratives. Of course, all children imagine, and everybody has a fund of stories about self. But theater people often have two: one story fit for public consumption and approval and another darker, grittier tale fit for late-night confession.

Nicky's mother's story was a disturbing one. Betty Crombie Pennell had trained as a secretary in London, according to Sebastian Breaks, a boyhood friend of Nicholas, whose mother Rosie was Betty's comrade. A well-kept secret was that both young women had applied for and been turned down for entrance to the Royal Academy of Dramatic Art. Certainly dramatic (even raucous) their lives were. Betty eventually went to Devon on the heels of a broken heart. One day a yacht sailed into the harbor at Brixham and the helmsman would become Nicholas' father, (Peter) Follett Russell Croker Pennell. He was weak, a man who'd never been trained to do anything, but he had money and the yacht, on which the two lived during the early months of their marriage. Eventually, he joined the Royal Air Force and remained in the bottom ranks. Betty, on the other hand, wanted a higher scale of living and after the war, there were bitter rows and an even more bitter divorce in 1945, the conclusion of eight years of marriage.

Nicky was wounded by the divorce, and Betty moved the family, which now included younger brother Robin, into a small cottage near Broadsands. Here she kept heart and soul alive by raising chickens, ducks, and geese and growing a vegetable garden, all of which provided golden produce during the war. Betty was a worker. She had "standards" and she wanted her boys to grow up to be gentlemen. She claimed a heritage tenuously linked to the gentry (more so for Nicky than for herself). She was one of the shipwrecked middle class during the war, who measured her life out in coffee spoons and, more importantly for the boys, in pints of lager.

The female society that Nicky described included Betty and her friends Lupin, Rosemary Spring (Sebastian's mother), and Patty Poos. They were hard drinkers and heavy smokers who frequently joined the darts tournaments at the local pub. Occasionally, the children would be parked at the pub before Sunday lunch. They would wait with a glass of lemonade until they got bored and went home without their mother. Drink brought out the stentorian cynic in Betty, and Sebastian Breaks described her as a kind of local *monstre sacre*, one who could make vicious but memorable pronouncements with razor-edged accuracy. Young Nicholas' relationship to her was largely propitiatory. He brought her gifts, attempted to please her, but was often running to Sebastian wondering what he'd done to deserve her painful censure.

Eventually, Betty re-married to a kind man, Gerry Milton, and although the moving-around-Devonshire did not cease, at least the houses were larger and more fashionable. Gerry's family had owned cinemas around Stoke-on-Trent. He was a licensed pharmacist, an unsophisticated man, yet he wanted very simple things in life beyond tending to his shop. Gerry brought stability to the boys and also siblings, two of his own children, Guy and Hillary, whom Betty raised. There were always trips to the seaside, the dogs that Betty raised, the pageant at the Crompton Castle where Betty played a peasant and the boys had speaking parts, and also child's play, in which Nicky was the initiator of great schemes.[9]

Then there was kindergarten at Broadsands, and later The Downs School, a preparatory school which Nicky and Sebastian attended together. They had a brilliant kindergarten teacher named Miss Goodman ("She always encouraged my imagination. She had hair right down to her ankles")[10], and he learned to read early on with her help. Robin added that Miss Goodman taught the importance of self-presentation, especially through language: One did not say "Buvvey Tracey but rather Bo-vey Tracey" and the birds were "plo-vers not pluvvers." Miss Goodman was a kind of Miss Jean Brodie at work. There is one story of Betty taking Nicky to Windy Corners to the schoolbus and later on the teacher calling to find out how Nicky was feeling since he hadn't been at school—turns out he stayed at the bus stop all day long, entertaining little old ladies with his fantastic tales as they waited for their rides!

Robin recollects the anticipation of Nicholas returning from public school for the summer, and later the return of the prodigal wearing a bit thin as Nicky began organizing them into building sets and making costumes for plays he wrote, such as *The Purple Peacock*, where Nicky played the larger roles and the rest of the children were spear-carriers, assuming the minor roles. Once, Nicky took his siblings across the fields and had them stand on top of a hedge. He convinced them that the wind had not bowed down the corn in front of them (which it had) but that the corn had been arranged in the shape of a hammer and sickle, a signal to a Russian spy to parachute into the field. They found an empty can, which became the poison container, the plan of the spy being to infect all the townspeople through the reservoir. The story continued with masses of sub-plots: "I always remember the excitement of rushing about and getting lathered up with all Nick's prompts."[11]

Nicky's future was miraculously insured by the money of a grand-dame grandmother, who would arrive in a chauffeur-driven car on Saturdays and take him to Della's Cafe, a tea-room with a small orchestra, where young Nicholas would request "The Teddy Bears' Picnic." She once took him to a location where you could see five counties (like Cecily Cardew in *The Importance of Being Earnest*). This grandmother paid for his education at Allhallow's, however, there was enough money to educate only the eldest son and not his brother Robin. Admission to Allhallow's required the submission of a genealogy of Crokers and Crombies and Folletts, the judges and bishops and vice-admirals that had preceded him in the family chain, among them "Edmund Burke, poet" and "The Beautiful Miss Croker," whose portrait had been done by Sir Thomas Lawrence.

Allhallows was the kind of place where the English sort out their class system early on and train young gents about manners, studying the classics, deprivation, and the correct wearing of the stiff upper lip. Such schools were privately funded and the students usually boarded there. Founded in 1614, Allhallows was located at Rousdon on Lyme Bay. The Prospectus told of attaining the land for the school through the personal efforts of "an Old Boy," one of the alumni. The school board featured the Earl of Devon and Viscount Sidmouth as well as an array of instructors in history, French, English literature, and physical sciences who had Honors degrees from Oxford and Cambridge. There was chapel, all the food was produced on the Home Farm. Specially-tailored grey tweed suits (with "all trouser pockets sewn up") were worn daily. Nicholas was detained here during the formative years until he was 18 in 1956.

In school, the younger Nicholas was rather solitary:

> . . . Imagination amongst one's peers was highly suspect. You had to be very careful to mask any imaginative existence.... I had to live very much inside myself in order not to open myself to the kind of cruelty children can inflict on other children. People who I was in school with [were] always incredibly surprised that I went into the theater because I was very mouse-like until about the age of 16.

Nonetheless, one of the advantages of this monastic establishment was small classes and empathetic teachers. Horace Hogg-Lee, "a big fat man," was a teacher who enjoyed putting on the kind of H.M. Tennant production that was playing in the West End. Hogg-Lee would cast himself in the lead while the boys played the supporting roles. Nicky remarked:

> Later on, when I was older, I met this wonderful actress Margaret Leighton in London. I was very shy and nervous and she said, "How are you?" and I said, "I'm fine, and oh, it's so good to meet you because I feel I know you already," and she said, "Why is that?" and I said, "Because I've played all your parts!" You see, I'd made a specialty of the Margaret Leighton roles in school.

Pennell also performed from Molière's *Le Bourgeois Gentilhomme* and read Shakespeare but did not perform it. He was required to memorize a great deal of poetry: "I couldn't tell you the Shakespeare play I acted last year... but the whole of 'The Shropshire Lad' and a lot of T.S. Eliot and the Georgian poets are still with me." He'd also read a great deal of Sassoon, which aided him much later in his performance of the play *Not About Heroes*. Sassoon lived on a farm in Devon, one of the many intersections this poet was to have in Nicky's life. The encouragement of a literature teacher named Thompson and a housemaster named Stone whetted his interest in reading poetry, "a great boon and a blessing, particularly coming into the verse plays." Another teacher was Dr. "Taffy" Evans, who taught Music Appreciation and wove another important strand into the schoolboy's life. The students had just returned from a school matinee performance of *Macbeth* and were listening to Beethoven's *Seventh Symphony* which suddenly inspired in Nicky's head the exchange between Macbeth and his wife as they plotted to kill Duncan.[12] Later on, playscripts and musical scores would have a certain creative conjunction in his ideas about acting. He often compared a Shakespearean text to a musical score.

The unwilling schoolboy wrote from Downs to "Mummy and Gerry" that "I have done the most wonderful thing, you probably won't believe it but [I] actually went up one in form, isn't it wonderful." In a letter which came from Allhallows later on,[13] the whole character of the handwriting had changed into a neat slanted script along with numerous "awfully's" (as in "Thanks awfully"). He wrote about a film at school called *The First of the Few* which was "about the Battle of Britain. The Star is Leslie Howard, do you remember him—he was killed in an air crash." (Nicky later had the role of a fighter pilot who "scrambled" for his Spitfire in the 1969 film *Battle of Britain*.) This letter from Allhallows School closes with a grown-up paragraph:

> "Well, that's all for now, give my love to the small boys and the sweet little girl whom I look down on now that I'm a public schoolboy! Also, my love to the two horrible pariah dogs with a kiss on the nose for each of them. My love to you both,

darlings, I'm lucky to have two such darling parents, thanks for everything."[14]

Report cards from Allhallows indicate that his interest in school improved considerably as time went on, and he even excelled at certain subjects. At age 15, he was doing best in English class with a "lively intelligence and zest," but hadn't quite developed the ability to focus and concentrate. His Form Master wrote, "He is an interesting boy to teach. His imagination is a fertile one, but he must discipline it: otherwise, it will be a handicap instead of the asset it should be—even in the acting profession." His report at age 17 demonstrated maturity and the development of leadership qualities with the English teacher assessing him "decidedly the best in this group; he brings an intelligent and appreciative mind to whatever is under discussion. Passionately keen and interested." The Housemaster noted a "general trend towards a greater stability" and the Headmaster added, "He has genuine interest in literature, drama and the arts generally. I hope he will find a career which will give it scope and at the same time enable him to make a reasonable living. The pitfalls are many. I wish him the best of luck." "The pitfalls are many" could be another allusion to Nicky wanting to enter the acting profession. Clearly, Nicky had discussed the possibility with his teachers.

When asked about whether or not his parents supported his going into the theater, the answer was qualified. (We can say with certainty this was not the career his maternal grandmother had in mind.) At first Gerry and Betty were flabbergasted and tried to impress upon him the importance of having security in his future—a lawyer, even an admiral, would have been more in line with their hopes. Betty urged a choice similar to her own: "Ma was fine, she said go ahead, she didn't think I'd be able to do it anyway…. but she insisted that I took a secretarial course so in fact I learnt typing and shorthand."

Nicky eventually attributed his becoming an actor to "a large dandelion clock with all those little seeds, and each seed had something written on it, and I happened to sniff when one that said 'actor' went by." This was his fanciful way of describing the ultimate choice, but the foundations for going into the theater profession were present in his traditional schooling and in Betty's proclivity for story-telling and personal drama.

III.
Youth And Observation Copied There

NICKY MADE APPLICATION to the Royal Academy of Dramatic Art in 1956 at age 18 and was accepted on his audition. However, he was not ready to commit to the work involved. Having been shut up in an English boarding school, he waded into London's diversions and almost drowned. Once he encountered a city as cosmopolitan as London, he was thrown into a large and sophisticated world. Drama school took a back seat—he did no work at the academy and very nearly lost his scholarship.

Just in time, an understanding principal at RADA, John Fernald, called him in and applied benign blackmail. He told Nicky that if he were willing to dedicate himself to a job in the theater and stick to it for awhile, Fernald would review the record at the end of the period of probation. Fernald got him a job at the Chesterfield Repertory Company as an assistant stage manager for about £10 a week. This meant working sixteen-hour days and also learning about building sets, painting props and lighting. The company motto was "Stay six days and see six plays." The job went on for nine months, and there was some acting involved:

> In my first professional role, I was playing Peter Cratchit in *The Christmas Carol* and waiting for my cue. The door of the green room opened. The actor

playing Scrooge was an inveterate practical joker, and although I knew full well I was not onstage until the second act, he said, "Nicholas! You're on!" Without pausing to think, I shot onto the stage and shouted, "Mother, mother, the goose is burning!" (The joke is that the leading man was Ronald Harwood, who went on to write *The Dresser*, a play I would later perform in.)

Nicky maintained that the Chesterfield experience was paramount to the rest of his career. He learned work discipline the hard way because his colleagues had high expectations and he would have been fired if he hadn't come through. He often learned on the run, on his feet. On the basis of the good word the Chesterfield people gave, Fernald subsequently re-admitted him to RADA.

Only later did Nicky realize at what an important juncture he was entering the profession. He was training and doubling parts with Tom Courtenay, Brian Bedford, Albert Finney, and Peter O'Toole, who were at RADA at about the same time he was.[15] George Bernard Shaw had left half his estate (the Shaw Bequest) to fund students who otherwise wouldn't have had the chance to enter acting training. So Pennell, ordinarily an "anyone-for-tennis?" kind of gentleman player, was suddenly confronted with this tough working-class power at a time when the culture was undergoing tumultuous change. This was reflected in John Osborne's *Look Back in Anger*, which exemplified a trend toward experimentalism in dramatic writing and generated plays that eventually replaced drawing-room comedies as the staple of theatrical fare.

The transition also enforced a different way of looking at characterization for actors: "If you wanted to keep your head up, you had to find a different kind of motive." Nicky's generation formed the nucleus of the transformed Royal Shakespeare Company under Peter Hall and afterwards became the mainstays at the Royal National Theatre. The artists that came out of the late fifties and early sixties prompted the theater scene to change radically: "Therefore, the way one had to approach the work [of acting and performance] also changed." The training for classical theater—Shakespeare, Restoration comedy, the Greeks—was not abandoned but was integrated into the hyper-realism that became fodder for new plays. Stanislavsky was metamorphosed into an acceptable system for "realistic" characterization in Shakespeare.

Other major contacts Pennell made at RADA were John Broome, Peter Barkworth, Clifford Turner, and David Giles, all of whom were to set standards he followed throughout his career. John Broome, originally trained in ballet and classical dance, became more dissatisfied with the limitations of those art forms and moved over into developing modern dance and movement for theater productions, joining his interest in acting with his talent in dance. He finally evolved a point of view about stage movement, fight choreography, and the management of crowd scenes as part of a conscious overall production design. He worked for nine years at RADA and also with the Royal Shakespeare Company. Broome ultimately settled in Stratford, Ontario, partly as a result of some serious persuasion by Pennell.

Peter Barkworth was an influential teacher to whom Nicky attributed the kernels of character analysis he used throughout his life: "He was an astonishing man who taught me about the truthfulness of acting, of not creating 'theatrical things' but finding out how the character's experience paralleled your own." Clifford Turner was the forerunner of people like Kristin Linklater and Patsy Rodenburg, voice teachers who acknowledged his work because he put the foundations in place from which later training could be established. David Giles eventually worked with Nicky in *The Forsyte Saga.*

After he'd graduated, Pennell was somewhat critical of his RADA experience:

> A drama school *per se* is so incredibly competitive. If you're insecure in any way it takes years to get over the experience. I know it took me a long time to get over the things that happened to me in drama school—mainly because there was always that sense of competition, and I don't think that is a good thing at all.[16]

Although RADA was clearly losing its "finishing school" reputation and had changed hands from Sir Kenneth Barnes to the more capable Fernald, Nicky felt there were professors there who were "either past it or who should never have been teaching there in the first place." He'd spent two years at RADA and stated that he could have learned what it had to offer in three months. Certainly, he considered his hands-on experience in stage work by far the most valuable part of his training.

By the time he left school, he had worked in two different generations of theater, the Chesterfield-Rep group where people went to rehearsal in hats and gloves and addressed each other as "Mr." or "Miss," and the newer discuss-as-you-act style epitomized by the Royal Shakespeare Company, where actors had or affected a working-class accent, attended rehearsal in jeans, and analyzed the script along with the director.

Nicky's first job out of school was in musical comedy, the old-style revues done in the West End and in the regions. Partly because he looked a bit like pop singer Adam Faith, he was cast in *Carry On Laughing* in Bournemouth, at the end of the pier:

> One of the dangers of rep was that you had a bag of tricks and... you could pull them out to enliven a performance. You had no time to investigate the character. The week was spent learning the lines and memorizing the moves because that was all you had time for. So you could fall into some bad habits.
> The value of the lesson was that.... you learned about timing and technique. You learned what it means to "be in the moment," which means to be absolutely committed to the person you are playing, completely in character, even if it is only 3 minutes long. You can't just put on a funny hat and do it, you have to... find the reality of that character.

Much later in life, this gift was praised by a grumpy critic in a review of a 1980 production of *Henry VI*:

> [Nicholas Pennell] is cornering Stratford's baddies. In *Henry VI*, he first plays the Duke of Suffolk with an evil slickness that makes his courting of Queen Margaret one of the play's clearest, most enjoyable scenes, and then limps on stage as Gloucester, the future Richard III, and very nearly hobbles away with the rest of the play. He is also one of the few actors onstage with enough technique to really make a character stick in the short time each is given on stage in this production.[17]

The repertory experience at "the end of the pier" was where many actors began their careers and, as lore has it, the weaker ones stayed there. Nicky enjoyed the work and gleaned experience and technique from it:

> When there was high tide and a rough sea in Bournemouth, [the waves] hit the underside of the theater and there was so much noise that the audience couldn't hear what we were saying. Which is probably just as well because it was pretty sophisticated London revue—a bit above their heads water-wise, I should say.

Nicky's life in London also was punctuated with music. He had, as a child, occasionally stayed with his Great-Aunt Ethyl, who was a painter and "a rather remarkable old girl who strode about in britches all the time and wore very odd hats."[18] Although eventually killed by a bomb, she had taken him to his first concerts. When he began his acting career, a cousin who was a pianist got him a room in the London Music Club, a lovely old Victorian house in Holland Park run by Adela Armstrong. It was a hostel for musicians such as Yehudi Menuhin who often rehearsed in the large music rooms prior to giving concerts at the Albert Hall. Nicky was thus tuned in to the music community and attended a great many recitals and concerts. Eventually he began to make more and more connections between text and music, an idea which transferred into his own vocabulary of performance while working with Michael Langham later on in Canada, who also referred to the playscript as a musical score.

In 1961, a friend at the London Music Club knew a producer and got him an audition for a play called *Masterpiece* which featured an actor who played in a number of films including *The Red Shoes*—Anton Walbrook. This was one of the first times Nicky had watched a veteran performer at work. Walbrook came in to the first reading of the play with the skeleton of the character:

I watched him all the way through rehearsals, he gradually put the musculature onto the bone and then the flesh... with the absolute precision of a surgeon. I was playing a small part but it was riveting to observe the process as I did then, at that stage in my career.

Nicky felt that Walbrook, all but forgotten now, was his link to nineteenth-century continental European acting. Although not officially an apprentice, he would later espouse the idea of mentoring, of younger actors having the opportunity to observe the old masters at work and to study their technique.

During the early 1960s Nicky's work consisted of small parts with one notable season at Pitlochry Festival Theatre in 1961. Television offered considerably better roles than the stage, with a part in a Maigret mystery, a role in *Tunnell Trench* for Granada Television, and Alyosha in *The Brothers Karamazov* for BBC-TV. In the middle 1960s, he picked up four lucky roles that got him some attention. He did a season at the Oxford Playhouse, where new talent is duly vetted by London producers—Dapper in *The Alchemist*, and Frederick in Anouilh's *Romeo and Jeannette*—where he developed a crush on his co-star Judi Dench. Within Nicky's romanticized ideas about marriage (since his experience of his parents' marriage had been fairly negative), he fancied that he was in love with Dench.

The role of Charles Darnay in a BBC remake of *Tale of Two Cities* and a soap opera called *Emergency Ward 10* provided more exposure as did an ironically lucky play, *The Vortex*, in which he played the role Noel Coward originally performed. The character of Nicky Lancaster knew about an affair his mother had, and the script also subliminally hinted at the son's homosexuality. Nicky told Sebastian Breaks about the role, "I find it very easy to do," a comment Breaks assumed was about Betty's escapades.[19] This production was the one seen by Granada Television's John Murphy, the director of *The Forsyte Saga*.

Early on, BBC Drama established a high standard of television production by using promising writers such as Tom Stoppard, Hugh Whitemore, Giles Cooper, and Harold Pinter. Both BBC and Granada Television produced some truly remarkable dramas in the sixties and seventies, just at the point in time when the general public was able to afford television sets. Amazingly, Nicky had appeared in over 200 television programs by the time he got to Canada, a considerable credential for someone in his middle thirties.

The Forsyte Saga, made in 1967, however, was the luckiest strike of all and established him as one of the young promising stars in England. It was originally targeted for a BBC2 (which had just started) television series because BBC Drama judged it would have a fairly limited audience appeal. The series had 26 episodes, was done in black and white, and cost £260,000 to make. A year later, it was released on BBC1 and the madness began. Cricket matches finished early, and church services on Sunday evenings were canceled because the program was so popular that it cut into attendance while it was on the air. It was rebroadcast in 1970 and shown in the U.S. in 1975.

The Forsyte Saga was an important social and entertainment phenomenon, a family epic which covered over fifty years of history and required 150 speaking parts. The leads were required to age in their roles; the patriarch Soames Forsythe goes from age 26 to age 71, with the aid of make-up and skilled acting, of course. The series won 4 BAFTA awards for Best Drama Series, Best Actor (Eric Porter as Soames), Best Actress and Best Designer.[20] It was also the first successful collaboration of British television talent (largely imported from British theater) and American corporate money, a paradigm not only imitated thereafter but eventually giving rise to the Public Broadcasting System's *Masterpiece Theatre*, a Sunday-night program which largely offered British costume dramas. Both of these events in the popular media literally recuperated historical drama (partly because of the stellar quality of the acting as well as the accuracy of the sets, costumes, and make-up) and spawned a number of popular creations such as *Upstairs, Downstairs*. With a viewing audience of 15 million in Britain and a worldwide audience of 160 million in 45 countries, such offshoots are perhaps no surprise.[21]

The television program serialized the six John Galsworthy novels about a property-conscious upper middle-class English family set against the backdrop of Victorian and Edwardian life, spanning the years between 1879 and 1926. Kenneth More played Jolyon Forsyte, the son who forsook wife and family for his German mistress and caused the family estrangement. Eric Porter was the lawyer Soames Forsyte whose wife Irene, played by Nyree Dawn Porter, had an affair with a penniless architect. Amidst this family turmoil, the story also followed the doomed relationships of the Forsyte children, notably the marriage of the rich and spoiled Fleur (Susan Hampshire) to the long-suffering Michael Mont (Nicky's role), an aristocratic socialist. The story thoroughly explored issues such as class and privilege, which appealed to the Sixties generation, and simultaneously unearthed a nostalgia for the Edwardian period and the kind of transitional social progress it eventually displayed, including the changing national attitudes to war and the early stirrings of the women's movement.

The cast was to yield lifelong friends for Nicky. Susan Hampshire became a chum, and Margaret Tyzack (who played Winifred in the series) later performed with him in Stratford, Ontario. Eric Porter, who preceded Nicky in death by three months, was a trusted friend. Porter had begun his life as a Shakespearean actor with Donald Wolfit and was known to rival both Olivier and Gielgud in a number of his stage portrayals. The series took an entire winter to show and, by the end of it, a number of acting careers were permanently established. Porter received a suitcase full of letters from people who empathized with Soames, a character with a severe exterior but a sensitive soul.

No one realized what an explosion the program would make. The series generated a number of fanciful features in the tabloids and Sunday supplements, articles which boosted Nicky's career. A ladies' journal displayed photos of cast members dining on the lawn just outside the rehearsal rooms, and even listed what foods they enjoyed: "Nicholas' picnic passion comes from a childhood spent in Devon with picnics packed into a huge laundry basket."[22] Another article in the *Radio Times* bemoaned the number of times he'd been "pinched" by adoring fans in public. He added, "There's one girl in Scotland who must be practically bald. She keeps sending me a lock of hair and says, 'Wear it next to your heart.'"[23]

Nicky and Susan Hampshire were asked to fly to Stockholm to promote the series in Sweden. They looked out of the airplane and saw crash barriers and hundreds of people gathered at the airport. The stewardess said that a major politician must have arrived, and she went to the cockpit to find out about the delay. She came back with an odd look on her face and asked him and Miss Hampshire to get ready to deplane. It was Nicky's one very heady taste of being a star. Another time he was eating in a restaurant on holiday in Zagreb when he rather nervously felt everyone looking at his table. Finally, his companion motioned to the television set and there he was, appearing as Michael Mont and speaking a foreign language.

Much to Betty Pennell's pride and pleasure, her notable son was spotlighted in her hometown *Paignton News*, where the writer explained that Nicky was best known for his film and television work but had recently returned to the stage. Nicky confessed that live theater was his first love and emphasized his passion for the interaction with a live audience. He also commented that the Michael Mont part had advanced him: "It does mean that I don't have to accept every part that is offered me, but can pick and choose to a certain extent."[24] His career was off to a healthy start in Britain; he was making the right contacts and getting lots of visibility.

Along with work, of course, came money. In those days, the BBC paid upwards of £180 pounds a week, and that meant that Nicky could invest in some permanent digs. He acquired a flat in Callow Street in London, his portrait was painted, and he also got himself involved in a very permanent enterprise. He partnered with a young horticulturalist named John Williamson, who'd begun his training at Bath University but left because he'd wanted to specialize in herbs and the faculty there didn't cotton to that revolutionary idea.

The two young men purchased a cottage (there were three dwellings grouped together) at Tumbler's Bottom, at the bottom of Tumbler's Hill in Somerset. The house had formerly been workmen's cottages built in 1720 on the estate of Lord Hylton. They dug in and renovated the inside, the plan being to "do the overall basics, like plumbing, first. Then go through the whole thing room by room."[25] The cottage was positioned on two acres of land which contained a trout stream and the "Pennell Herbiary." All this information was laid out in an article in the Sunday supplement where Nicky was portrayed as a kind of country squire. Pennell "has obtained a special import license to bring certain herbs into Britain from other countries, notably France," kept a white cockatoo (named Beady, who spouted phrases like "You're a silly old beggar"), and intended to produce his own wine.[26] There was a less glossy companion article about Williamson making specialized curry powders at Tumbler's Bottom Herb Farm. In both articles, each fellow was called a bachelor (also

"Pennell is alone in his bit of Tumbler's Bottom"). Nicky was quoted as saying, "You know, if another part never offered itself, I'd be content to live here—waxing the bare boards until they shine... and glooming round the country auctions picking up [antiques] like this."[27]

Certainly, this was a period of great contentment for Nicky. How the division of labor got worked out, no one will ever know for sure, however, they had found a very solid relationship and that was a spur to create the business. Letters later on in 1974 revealed that Nicky was a director of the herb farm, and that John Williamson was developing a company that was beginning to succeed, hiring a gardener, creating catalogues and sending them out, eventually exhibiting the herbs in London at fairs.[28] Frequent visitors were Nicky's friends, Clare Showell, and Sebastian Breaks and his wife.

There were seances with candles and incense, glasses bouncing about, and speaking to people "who'd gone before." Such diversions were in concert with Nicky's interest in the afterlife, another thread in his fascination with shape-changing. There were also the famous Tumbler's Bottom Boxing Days, where Nicky made Black Velvets with Guinness and champagne, and John cooked, always a gourmet meal. A frequent visitor and good friend, Clare Showell was in training as a social worker and asked Nicky to visit the home for disturbed girls nearby, where she was working. *The Forsyte Saga* was one of the few television programs they were allowed to watch. He made two trips there and conversed with the fascinated young women about their progress and their lives.

Sebastian Breaks and his wife Anna rented one of the cottages for weekends in the country. They remembered this as one of the most enjoyable times of their young adulthood and told stories about Nicky and John hob-nobbing with the local nobility. A wide variety of interesting people, mostly theater friends, used to visit. A family saga made it possible for this period of equanimity in Nicky's life, for it is clear that his profits from the *Forsyte* serial helped a great deal to sustain the herb farm enterprise, although it must have been expensive to keep the Callow Street flat in London as well as the farm. Nicky's financial sense was never spectacular. Later in life, he lost sums of money by trusting the wrong people.

There lurked in the subconscious some cruel memories engendered by Betty, whose pointed tongue could deflate all Nicky's successes in a most blind-sided way. No matter how well-known Nicky became, it was impossible to meet Betty's precarious standards.

Although the role of Michael Mont in *The Forsyte Saga* certainly fit Nicky's good looks and reserved manner, it also type-cast Nicky as "a charming, kind, intelligent, perfect (really) young man, and I played that kind of role to death and eventually didn't want to play it any more." There were yearnings to "explore a larger palette, the richer aspect of humanity." Nevertheless, the first offer to go to Canada in 1972 was to play juvenile roles, Orlando in *As You Like It* and Young Marlow in *She Stoops to Conquer*. William Hutt had seen him performing Orlando at the Bristol Old Vic, which initiated an invitation to Stratford. Nicky told his agent that he'd done virtually no Shakespeare and that he'd like try it.

After one season, he returned to England. Jean Gascon, then the Artistic Director at Stratford, traveled there and asked him to return to Canada the following season for a revival of *She Stoops to Conquer*. Nicky began to demur but Gascon quickly offered *Pericles*, which had never been performed in Stratford, and so a second season was agreed to. *Pericles* was important because Gascon, who directed the show, "had an extraordinary Gallic flair for romance and for scale. He was astonishing, the Quebecois sensibility at its most attractive."[29] Also, Gascon made him take great physical risks as choreographer Patricia Arnold was hired to create movement for the storm sequence, the freeing-up work Nicky felt he sorely needed as an actor. *Pericles* was also Nicky's first full-blown classical-acting stage success and probably the role that would eventually remove him from England and the partnership with John Williamson. It was a magical production and a great success in Stratford and earned him a number of new fans.

In the meantime, a letter from England from Williamson dated 8 January 1974, which appeared to be written after Nicky had returned home for a short visit, probably a Christmas trip, indicated that Williamson was making his own life plans inclusive of Nicky:

> I... spoke with [director] Val May last week and [he] wished he had known that you were in England because there were some parts he would have offered you. So much for [Nicky's agent] Peter Brown - have you sorted out your percentage yet? Bet not! Well, he will offer you work when you return next Autumn.

Williamson added to this a very detailed account of a recent storm on the Tumbler's Bottom property and talked about the positive results of recent advertising which had him sending off seeds and increasing the number of curry packets he'd decided to offer for sale. There were also details about money—the enterprise was initially precariously funded through the Pennell family silver, loans from relatives, and investments from partners. Affection was expressed throughout for Nicky and anecdotes of family and friends amusingly narrated:

> John Heal came down last weekend and we had a pleasent [sic] luncheon with the Taylors. Talked about farting, a subject near to your heart. Billie's great story was when his brother tried to blow a candle out and the fart ignited and burnt his balls!

New Year was great fun. Neddy's turkey was 29 lbs. and lasted me a week. The last few meals were turkey curry which I gave to [Nicky and John's dog] Gimli - and that story about farting needs another chapter.

During Nicky's third season in Canada, with his English agent "getting rather shirty," Nicky explained to Jean Gascon that he really could not afford to be away from the London television work another year. Gascon replied, "What do you mean! Work is the theater!" Whereupon the role of Berowne was offered from *Love's Labour's Lost* plus a long tour to Australia. An offer Nicky couldn't refuse, Berowne was a meaty verse role (not prose like Orlando) and also a character who was immensely articulate, with great wit and style. Added to the package were those three months in Australia, along with William Hutt and Pat Galloway, in a company tour of Molière's *Imaginary Invalid* (aided by Gascon and with Tanya Moiseiwitsch as costumier). The group performed in Perth, Melbourne, Adelaide, and Sydney.

This tour was colorfully documented in a 1974 video called *The Players*, co-sponsored by the National Film Board of Canada and the South Australian Film Corporation. The decision was made to take a Molière play because it was cheaper to stage than a Shakespearean performance. Even though Hutt played a leading role, he also alternately bullied and cajoled the locals and the technical crews into providing more support. There were 157 hours of rehearsal and 125 performances to audiences who wildly applauded the actors.

The film showed the company in rehearsal, providing a taste of Jean Gascon's genial love for suggesting ideas to the company, "To rehearse is to enjoy." It pictured the actors at work and then partying (seventies-style) after the show was over. Nicky said in a voice-over, "Anyone who is an actor after [age] 30 must be slightly unbalanced. After you're 30, I think it is a sign of emotional immaturity." He was 36 on the occasion of this momentous pronouncement.

The trip was a bonding experience for these Stratford regulars. Long-term friendships were forged. They cavorted on the beach, rented a car, and saw the sights Down Under. Galloway described it as a sublime adventure:

> We'd all had far too much alcohol too soon in those days, so we decided to swear off the hard stuff and drink only white wine on the trip. Tanya did a drawing of the four of us, called "The Vile Quartet" which I still have hanging in the kitchen. My husband used to laugh about how we claimed we were so pure yet never mentioning how much wine had been consumed. Nicky was the first to break the pledge.... One of our managers took to calling him "The Glory That Was Greece," which was rather good because we were all slightly but not quite over the hill.
>
> Bill played the Invalid, Nicky's character had pimples painted all over him, and I was the maid.[30]

When he returned, Nicky was asked to join the Young Company in 1975, an experimental group made up of some Stratford regulars and a younger apprenticing cadre, assembled by arguably the most creative director the Stratford company had ever had, Robin Phillips. Phillips then extended an irresistible invitation: Nicky would share *Hamlet* with the fiery Richard Monette to be performed in 1976, presenting an exciting contrast between the romantic, poetic, fair-haired Nicholas and the angry, brooding, dark Monette.

By this time, Nicky had been doing three years of thinking about his work as an actor. There was this very serious consideration: At what other major theater venue could one get the kind of classical roles he was being offered? In an interview on the radio program *Stereo Morning* in 1979, he mentioned the luck of Gielgud and Olivier and Richardson with Lilian Baylis at the Old Vic as "they started in their twenties with the Romeo's and went rollicking straight through the canon, one after another—and then came back and did them again!" Canada had offered him a once-in-a-lifetime option while other talented young actors sat in England waiting years for the next plum role.

The chance to truly and completely train as a classical actor was the most important lure to the brave new world. Add to this an amazing stage to perform on, one he never wanted to be far from, plus a crew of loving and supporting friends and colleagues, and Stratford, Ontario, Canada, eventually won the geographical tug of war.

IV.
There's A Divinity
That Shapes Our Ends

WHEN NICKY TALKED ABOUT STRATFORD, there was this permeating sense of his love for it, springing from the knowledge that he was so much a part of it that he actually helped to shape it. The experience of working in a resident acting company brought with it a special kind of camaraderie borne out of accumulated experience and expertise in the same performance spaces. There was the potential of deeper and more probing discussions about performing in those theaters as well as about the craft of acting. One could adjourn with colleagues or even audience members to a tavern afterwards. Once the wall of competition was eroded, then conflicting ideas could be floated, and these explorations produced interesting conversations about what works and what doesn't work aesthetically, something local interviewers were very aware of. Beyond the sociability, of course, was the centrifugal force of the intellectual power it took to act in classical plays with playwrights of the caliber of Sophocles, Molière, and Shakespeare.

A chief enticement about Canada was that it wasn't England: The traditions of theater were not yet forged and locked into place, so that the Stratford Festival could, in the deepest sense, make its own rules. Most certainly, a pioneering spirit of enterprise has existed among actors and directors there. The dialogue between actors and administrators, although spiky at times, has always been open and has helped to balance the seasons' offerings, keeping classical plays even with popular and financially successful ones. Actors had input. The essential metaphor of Stratford, as William Hutt pointed out to Nicky shortly after his arrival, was that designer Tanya Moiseiwitsch had purposely configured the theater so that every walkway and every aisle led eventually to the stage.

Like a number of North American festivals, this one was founded by an energetic and divinely inspired eccentric, a man obsessed with an idea. Although it was indeed true that the small town of Stratford was already so named and had several streets called after Shakespearean characters, it was also true that, in financial desperation, it needed to re-tool its economic base away from repairing steam engines for the railroad. In 1952, local citizen Tom Patterson had the idea and wrote to a world-famous director of classical theater, Irishman Tyrone Guthrie, inviting him to oversee a festival in Stratford. A year later, with tremendous local community support and Patterson's leadership, the Festival opened in a large canvas tent with a production of *Richard III* by Alec Guinness playing the lead—a role, incidentally, that Guinness would probably never have been asked to play in England.

The idea took off, and today the Festival boasts 3 sizable theater spaces (one of them named after Tom Patterson) in addition to the Festival theater, which features a thrust stage insisted on by Guthrie and designed by Tanya Moiseiwitsch. This space is quite magical and first views of it are inspiring: It not only replicates the spirit of Shakespeare's Globe but also majestically accommodates epic theater. It has clearly inspired talented directors to great achievement.

The town has about its Victorian homes the solid burgher-like flavor one feels in *The Merry Wives of Windsor*. Entering it is like moving into the 1950s, offering a kind of secure nostalgia and friendliness. People vacation there because they can get out into the country and can still see stimulating professional theater. In fact, the great human issues the plays evoke are perhaps better contemplated around Lake Victoria, created by the River Avon, which surrounds a small island, complete with black swans and other wild birds tamed by tourists feeding them.

The Festival staff has determined that a large percentage of their audience is female, which is catered to by the merchants of Stratford with rows of businesses offering distinctly precious giftware and several excellent restaurants. It is important to remember that the Festival operates from an aggressively-sought subscription base, with about 5% of its budget supported from the Canadian government. Forty percent of its audience is American, mostly from Michigan and the Chicago area, and the remainder is Canadian. Although the repertory rarely reaches the "dangerous" or "uncomfortable" theater Nicky talked about, it is always characterized by rock-solid competence with a strong corps of artists and near-genius displayed in production design.

Stratford has an important historical status as well since it was the first professional theater of any size in Canada, so young people seeking to make careers in the theater vie to train there. Over the years, it has discovered and regularly featured the first generation of Canadian writers' work — Robertson Davies' *World of Wonders*, for example — and has also fostered a raft of world-class actors, many of whom have become international stars who did not settle in Canada — Christopher Plummer, William Shatner, and Lorne Greene, for example. Other actors of the stature of William Hutt, Martha Henry, Richard Monette, Kate Reid, Colm Feore, and Nicky himself, did.

The history of the artistic directorship of the Festival is as varied as the personalities who have held the position. It is a position which includes artistic decision-making, fundraising, socializing, and directing productions. Tyrone Guthrie was the first and headed the company from 1953-55. Britisher Michael Langham then took over the company, bringing it on through its formative decade in the late 1950s, stabilizing the Festival as Canada's premier theatrical institution and also fostering the growth of Canadian artists especially via offering long-term work contracts. French Canadian Jean Gascon's tour of duty was marked by extensive outreach activities, linking the company with Ottawa's National Arts Centre and with Quebec. The repertory at that time was not particularly experimental, but breaking new paths and avant-garde theatrical fare have not traditionally been the role of the Festival. Its audience, over the years, has been middle-class; that group has reciprocated with financial support. It has, in effect, voted at the box office.

From Nicky's point of view, the most important director was British-born Robin Phillips, a personality whose modes of management and artistry engendered a diametrically split set of opinions about him. Actors and designers either loved him or hated him, could either work with him or could not. Certainly, whether or not you supported Robin Phillips at any point in time was a political statement within the company.

Phillips brought unique methods of working with actors and generated very fine performances from them. He was also enormously keen on detail, whether it be in theater design or in directorial conception. If a pleat on a curtain hanging at the back wasn't quite right, it would drive him crazy until it was straightened. Actor Janet Wright stated:

> No one could "work the room" like he did—if an actor was not paying attention or was out of line, Phillips caught it and fixed it. The only time I've ever thought about a line (after rehearsal) and said to myself, "I'll punch that word instead of this one—I had such a small part in *King John* I thought

I had to do something—the next day, he said,
"What's that line again?" and I gave it, and he said,
"Don't help me." That's how smart he was. He
had an ear perfectly pitched for dialogue.
Robin had more energy than anyone in rehearsals.
He was always sitting down and getting back up
again, and he never missed anything. So it was
terrifying in a way that everyone always did their
best, because he was always on.[31]

Phillips also got involved with the personal psyches of
performers, knowing how and especially when to create from
an actor's psychological template. Naturally, these methods
would take their toll on him and on the company. When he
was hired as Artistic Director in 1975, he toured Canada for a
year, auditioning actors and making a reconnaissance of the
arts scene. When he left the Festival in 1980, he was physically
unstable and somewhat mentally ravaged because he had
given so much of himself to the institution.

Part of Phillips' strategy to convince the Board of
Governors that the Festival needed a second home (which
never actually happened)in a major Canadian city was to
offer a full season and a widely varied cultural series. In the
golden years of his reign, the sheer number of shows offered
was impressive, averaging 13 per season. His stage
conceptions were brilliantly original and linked Shakespeare
with twentieth century ideologies. The 1975 *Measure for
Measure*, with his signature Edwardian design-concept,
brought out the Freudian undertones of the play and became
a definitive performance of the play worldwide. Also, he
directed new pieces like *Virginia*, bringing an altogether
international flavor and sensibility to Stratford. Pennell
certainly felt that Phillips' ideas influenced him more than
any other director, inspiring his best work on any stage.

Canadians occasionally feel that they are overshadowed

by British theater and by American theater (all radically different in tone and temper from one another). Of course, the Royal Shakespeare Company, especially the first two decades after Peter Hall took it over in 1958, led all of the theater world in terms of conceptualizing productions and setting the standard of "relevant" Shakespeare. Both Canadian and American producers of Shakespeare were influenced by trends in the RSC which, nowadays, is not necessarily considered the pivotal maker of fashion. The Canadian sense of self-consciousness probably generated from within the country rather than without. John Hirsch (the Artistic Director who followed Phillips) used to tell the wry story (reported by Stephen Ouimette) of two boiling lobster pots, one from the United States and the other from Canada. The lid must be kept tight on the American pot because they would all scramble out; the lid must also be kept tight on the Canadian one because if one lobster got out, the others would pull it back in! Most of the English-speaking world saw the Festival as the flagship of North American Shakespeare but perhaps more important than that, an entity in its own right, far different from any of the other international theater venues.

What was the appeal of this theater setting for Nicholas Pennell? Why would a man who had turned down an offer from Alec Guinness to do a season at Chichester because he had a movie bid—go to Canada and eventually make his home there? What kind of enchantments seduced him to this place? After all, the town of Stratford was isolated from other cultural centers. Despite its being two hours from Toronto, in many ways it didn't have to play Toronto's game of competing in a major art market. Nevertheless, the isolation bothered Nicky because he was accustomed to the many cultural and musical diversions of the most interesting city in the world, London. One of his complaints was about the lack of stimulation, especially in terms of seeing other theater productions, and also not having access to the BBC.

Nevertheless, for much of the time at Stratford, the work itself was compensation: "We were rehearsing as a company totally in private in the middle of winter in one room and all of the company were appearing in both plays, and that [focus] had an extraordinary concentration to it. It was marvelous."[32] Since the geographical location also required that actors live in Stratford for roughly nine months of the year, a microcosm of togetherness and support was created because the energies were directed at the work product, at making something artistically viable. This strategy had many advantages over the standard commercial model of producing theater. For one thing, rehearsals were more productive when actors knew one another. Ensemble work emerged more quickly, and the stress and extra time it took to get to know new colleagues was considerably mitigated:

> One of the joys of Stratford is that you get to work with people over a period of time, and you get to grow and change together "in choir" as you explore. It saves a great deal of time… [as opposed to] starting over each time with people you haven't met or you haven't worked with for some time— which takes a week to 10 days for you to adapt.… Whereas [in Stratford] you walk through that vulnerability—it's accepted.[33]
>
> Rehearsals—I mean, it's not just performance— to have a good rehearsal day is an astonishing thing, a gift. Although it's very nice to have audiences applauding out there and to have that relationship which is essentially what one does it for anyway! But some of the days that we spent on *King John*, for instance, were so satisfying—and you know that you've really achieved some form of originality, some form of newness.

Nicky loved the actor's process and was very involved in it. An artist should absorb and reject during rehearsal: That is the essence of the creative process for performers. At Stratford, there was time to do so because the rehearsal periods were long and fruitful. There was time for voice and body workshops, which at different times over the years have been required. Nicky believed that continued training was absolutely essential. In 1981, he stated,

> One thing I find very exciting is that this year we have a lot of apprentices and journeymen. For the first time now we have a contract whereby the classes are obligatory. So that younger members of the company have to go to classes and do warm-ups... . I'm teaching text this year to the apprentices so that I feel very involved with the younger members of the company.[34]

He worked with John Broome to regularize these ideas and was key in hiring voice professionals to do workshops for the company on a regular basis. Pat Galloway echoed these sentiments in an interview featuring herself and Nicky about English citizens performing abroad: "We also get a lot of extras such as coaching in voice and movement... ."[35] Ongoing training would not be one of the fringe benefits for actors working in most commercial venues.

An actor also had a great deal of economic security at Stratford because the contract covered the months from February to November of each year. S\he did not have to travel around to various theaters or capitulate to other pressures to pay the rent. (During Nicky's time there, Government subsidies did supplement the Festival budget, more so than they ever would in the U.S.) Nicky had a small but persistent tax bill with England's Inland Revenue that he was capable of eliminating with the help of a steady income.[36]

Furthermore, if an actor made his\her permanent home with the company, as a great many do in Stratford, there were other major benefits. An actor could build up a corpus of work, an *oeuvre*. This was not only personally satisfying but established a foundation in experience and information. It also helped in training other actors because there were established mentors who knew the rules, had learned to use the performance spaces and could pass on that experience and technique to other performers.

The values of the company idea were far-reaching and interlocking, which created gains for both the group and the individual. An actor could graduate from one line of acting to another, could move from the juvenile parts, as Nicky did, to the meatier character roles, from Marlow and Orlando to Hamlet, Iago, Angelo, Lear's Fool, King John.

About Iago, critic Gina Mallet exclaimed, "This is the first time Pennell plays a baddie, and he flowers as never before."[37] In fact, the breadth and range of characters that Nicky played was astonishing for someone to have achieved in a lifetime, let alone at his age. His work occasionally spawned the remark that he was too good an ensemble player to be a leading man. He had reached the Stanislavskian ideal of being so much a part of the play that the audience was seeing the play and not the star, hearing the text and not the performer. When he played the smaller character roles in Molière (roles which were assigned to offset leading roles during the season), audience members occasionally did not recognize him onstage.

Interestingly enough, an actor could even become a director, could change functions or add functions. A number of actors, notably Brian Bedford, Richard Monette, Marti Maraden, Douglas Campbell and others, initiated and/or furthered their directing careers on Festival stages.

Nicky knew that the acting of Shakespeare could change very rapidly and indeed had undergone significant shifts in performance styles, from the declamatory to the more realistic mode of verse speaking and character creation:

> I had to free myself from the kind of theatre I'd been trained in. I was at RADA in the fifties when it was just on the change from being a finishing school. Vocally and to a certain extent physically, I'd been trained to work the classics in a certain way. That has been very much removed here over the years, especially under Robin Phillips' direction when there was a much more naturalistic approach to text: One has also had to find not a mid-Atlantic but a slightly less-than-Oxford English sound—I tend to flatten some vowel sounds purely so that I don't distance the [North American] audience.[38]

Stratford was known for its mix of British, Canadian, and American dialects within Shakespearean productions, but here Pennell felt it important to conform somewhat to the local idiom so that his accent would not be a barrier for audience members and thus break the illusion or pop them out of the play unnecessarily.Nicky also recognized that the audiences in Canada were advancing his abilities as an actor. Working with a variety of performer-spectator configurations is one of the fastest and most useful ways to train actors and make them more flexible:

> Also this is a vast country, and people from many backgrounds come a long way to this theater (which is really the only major classical theater in North America doing the classics over three-quarters of the year) so that audiences change radically over the course of a summer, and the reactions to plays vary tremendously.

Another point is that 50 per cent of the audience don't know the play at all. That pays off in spades for actors, because unlike England where you have a lot of people who look on Shakespeare as their own personal property and make references fifty years back, here you have the staggering sense of people not knowing what is going to happen and so they identify and get drawn into the plays.[39]

There were two other considerable gains for every actor in the company. The first was the opportunity to work with a variety of talented directors. Stratford had been blessed in its Artistic Directors, from Sir Tyrone Guthrie to the present. Actors like Galloway and Pennell were able to work with the gifted Michael Langham, the romantic sensibility of Jean Gascon, the dark visionary John Hirsch, and the intellectual sinew of Robin Phillips. Consistent guidance and mentorship on this level of professionalism was indeed rare. Furthermore, the technical support in the Festival followed the dictum of "only the finest will do." The Stratford Company consistently had the highest standard possible in production values, featuring the foremost designers in the world. Tanya Moiseiwitsch, Desmond Heeley, Leslie Hurry, and Ming Cho Lee, for example, returned to the company year after year. The Festival actors always commented about the lavishness of the costumes and the spectacular qualities of technical work carried out at the Festival. It is a great boon for actors to have that level of design excellence supporting their work.

Many of these artistic advantages, in turn, fed into the company's mission and into its collaborative endeavor. Enforced training and refresher courses created readier, more stabilized actors who set a standard for quality. Individual plays could have a growth pattern. Instead of needing to have reached what Nicky called (citing Mrs. Malaprop) "the pineapple of perfection" on the first night (as a play had to do in New York, just to stay open), the production could develop during the season:

> One of the most important things about Stratford is that the performance you see at the opening is probably not the performance you'll see in August or September... . Any good director will allow growth to exist within a play... in different directions, in ways that are valid and truthful and hopefully exciting. You'd go bananas if the first night was the peak. You'd either go completely over the top or you'd sink down from that.... One of the nice things about the repertory situation is that the play will change. Certain things will disappear and other things will appear. Because one isn't playing the play every night, one is only playing two or three performances of it a week... . so that other productions will feed on the primary production.[40]

When asked whether or not the director usually helped this growth process, Nicky responded:

> I think it comes mostly from the actors. Derek Goldby, who's directing *Wild Oats* [in 1981] said a very interesting thing in rehearsals.... "at present you must listen only to me—I don't want you to listen to anybody else. What anybody else says doesn't count.... I will release the play when we open. That is my time to let you go, and then the play becomes yours"... .I think that's probably true.... once you reach the opening, the play has become, well, first of all the playwright's, but also the actors'.[41]

In consequence, the company was able to commit to a unique or radical interpretation and to stick with it. "The size of the failure should be measured by the size of the risk" is one maxim that Nicky articulated to deal with a production that had artistic merit but was not as bankable as hoped. He steadfastly maintained that the company should never cease to risk. Artistic Director John Hirsch proclaimed, in 1985:

> While it is true we represent a valuable commodity within the tourism industry, we never must lose sight of the fact that, above all, we are an artistic and educational entity whose principal function must be to feed the spirit and the soul.[42]

Such sentiments you would not hear often in New York or London.

Finally, the company was able to commit part of its resources to a teaching and outreach function, an important component of the Festival mandate. The Young Company, begun by Phillips in 1975, set up a situation where younger actors could work in plays as apprentices to a few older, more seasoned performers. The idea was to offer concentrated hands-on experience which younger actors would not ordinarily have with classical plays, particularly Shakespeare. The result began to emerge in the late 1970s and early 1980s when the middle layer of artists in the company grew to be enormously capable and supportive, something absolutely essential for a successful Shakespearean repertory. The policy insured a continuity of acting excellence and provided for the emergence of new talent within the cry of players.

If all of this begins to sound as if it mirrored Shakespeare's company, indeed there were operational parallels. The paradigm of the Stratford Festival was drastically different from the usual commercial model, where a group of theater professionals gathered together for eight weeks, worked toward opening night, and then disbanded (sometimes never to meet again), letting the actors carry the show as long as it made money. The Festival was also different from England's Royal Shakespeare Company because it had a longer continuity of resident actors and a strong commitment to the Canadian cultural milieu, to generating a distinctly Canadian theater scene as well as creating Canadian artists, both as actors and playwrights.

In 1980 and 1981, a series of incidents occurred that were to shake the foundations of the Festival and to involve the acting company, especially long-termers like Nicky. Robin Phillips resigned, after managing and directing six years of rich theatrical fare, including major productions and an accompanying arts festival of world-class talent. Phillips informed the Board of Governors that he was leaving and a rather ineffectual search for a new Artistic Director ensued. The company put forward a group of four company members (the "Gang of Four")[43] to manage the Festival. The Board of Governors rejected this gesture and made it known that it was considering a renowned British director, John Dexter. His pre-nomination lit a fuse under heretofore concealed issues among the performers. There was the also the feeling that the actors had not been included in selecting the candidate, and Dexter became the target for smoldering nationalistic sentiments. The Canadians in the company were tired of having "imports" foisted off on them—too long, they felt, had English actors and directors been called in to bolster the box office and to make decisions for a group which ought to be mostly Canadian. Actors' Equity refused to approve Dexter's candidacy and John Hirsch, a Canadian standing ready in the wings, was eventually put into the directorship to succeed Phillips.[44]

What was interesting about "the debacle and the whole kind of heave-around" was Nicky's reaction to it, outlined in a detailed way in an interview by Canadian Ivor Novello on

CBC on June 17, 1981. One of the places where the Canadian consciousness meshes so closely with the English consciousness is in the propriety of speaking one's own mind. That quality was amply demonstrated in Nicky's outspokenness in the interview, and also in the young-Turk quality of the commentary.

The interview began with Novello asking whether or not the turn of events could have been avoided. With lawyer-like precision and absolute fearlessness, Nicky dissected the situation:

> .... after the opening of *Coriolanus* last night, I went to a party at which there were several members of the Board [of Governors]. One of them came up and said the play reflected the mob attitude of the actors in the General Meeting in December [of 1980]. This was said with a kind of smirk. I said, yes, and I think you risked far more than a dislodging of the Board.... There was a point when we might very well have come down from the stage and torn you limb from limb.[45]

Nicky insisted in the interview that the seeds for the revolt "were sewn in the early part of the seventies" when there was a "determination to govern the stage via the box office," as if high revenues insured good drama onstage. Someone was brought in to raise the level of the administration (Nicky does not name names here), and that move suppressed the artistic end of the enterprise. Robin Phillips, in turn, had sought to "re-adjust that balance," to return to a period of quality theater rather than theater which would merely sell tickets.

Novello suggested that the infighting and bad publicity worldwide was detrimental to the Festival and asked the potentially combustible question, whether or not a Canadian theater should be limited to Canadian artists or if it should be

"truly international and include artists from other countries."
Nicky made the case that the media had fanned those
attitudes into flames: "I don't think [the issues] were for one
minute nationalist." He carefully explained that the
directorate of four people—Urjo Kareda, Martha Henry, Pam
Brighton, and Peter Moss—had been backed by the theatrical
company (the actors and designers) 100%. They realized that
Robin Phillips was leaving the company and they all needed
to get on with the work, so they supported the Gang of Four,
who were, after all, nominated from their ranks. Then the
Board dismissed them. In retaliation, Canadian Actor's
Equity vetoed hiring Englishman John Dexter, and the
Canadian government consequently refused to issue him a
work permit:

> It was a crisis of confidence in the operation, and
> I shall continue to believe that.... It was... a
> decision that had to do with the dismissal of
> people [the Gang of Four] who had been working
> here in Canadian theater for a number of years.
> And I think that's important.[46]

That year, a number of the regular company did not return,
which spawned a variety of rumors. Nicky contended that the
fact that there were fewer regulars in the 1981 season had to
do with contracts being offered unusually late that year and
so the season offered only 50% of the number of plays
ordinarily produced by the Festival: "I don't think there [was]
any deliberate new understanding that we've got to go with
an entirely new company because we've got to get rid of old
things"[47], i.e., eliminate members of the old company.

Nevertheless, the issue of non-Canadian "imports" had
been raised. The first Artistic Director was British, and British
artists like Maggie Smith had often been invited in to shore up
ticket sales. On these issues, Nicky clarified his stand:

I think if one's talking about Maggie Smith that's
something else again. She's a very great actress,
at the height of her powers. When she was
working at Stratford and I played with her, I think
I learned probably more from her than I did from
any other actor . . . . Of course we should have
people like that, because they should be playing
Shakespeare and certainly at Stratford—but I don't
like the import for the import's sake.[48]

He added emphatically, "I don't think nationalism ought
to be allowed in the theater. I believe that on a positive rather
than a negative basis."[49]

Of course, Nicky was born in England, and he'd had first-
hand experience with pro-nationalist sentiments:

. . . My very first year here in the winter I went
into Toronto to see a play.... We went into the bar
afterwards, and I was standing there and I half-
turned and saw two actors who had been in the
play. I was about to say, "Congratulations," and a
very chilly voice said, "Oh, to be in England now
that England's here.".... There was a very
understandable attitude because the Stratford
Festival had brought an awful lot of English
people here (however, what reputation I'd made
I made in television and not in theater). I think
probably in the long run one of the reasons I
decided to become a Canadian citizen was that I
felt I just couldn't go on being here without
making some commitment to this theater which
sits in this country and is part of this country.[50]

Nicky also worked tirelessly to promote a pro-Canadian
consciousness and lineage within the company. Certainly

some of this spirit of reformation was partly a result of the rest of the world community having its consciousness raised, sometimes painfully, in the liberal political climate that was a spill-off of the late 1970s.

Nicky felt that it was important that all involved, including the media, get the fury out, get the anger spent, and then get on with "the work." He insisted that Stratford was not about personalities and changes in the Artistic Directorship, and people should not lose sight of essential goals:

> A theatrical event that happened with *Coriolanus* last night was that people were forced to say this is good! Damn politics, damn everything else! Finally, what happened on the stage was important enough for people to be excited despite themselves.[51]

What we see here is a man who had given his all to support the premier theater of Canada. When it was threatened, and the central purpose of creating theater that appealed to the imagination and to the life of the mind was endangered, he stood up and said so. His analysis was clear-sighted and he saw beyond personal vindictiveness. In the end, he was an amalgamation of young rebel and company man.

It is also important to note that Robin Phillips was taking on the directorship of a theater in London, Ontario, and that Nicky had the option to join him. Nicky explained:

> "My loyalty lay to Stratford. To the theater. To Tanya's [Moiseiwitsch] and Tony Guthrie's idea of the theater and that it went beyond. I have great personal affection and gratitude for Robin, but I felt that I had to stay with the Festival."[52]

He went on to say that the same decision faced everyone in the company and that as he left in January of 1981 to tour *Virginia* in England, a tour on which he had offers to work there as well, "for the first time since I'd come to Canada, I was going back at a time when I did not know what my personal future would be or the future of the [Festival] theatre would be." There was not yet, in the early 1980s, a clear choice of leader in Stratford and even some danger that the theater could close.

Nicky's sense of politics was activist. He served on the Actor's Committee from 1981-1985 and chaired it in 1983. Along with other committee members, he worked to improve the communication lines between the Board and the company. This committee also urged senior members of the company to avail themselves of post-graduate training, so the group was open to self-criticism and self-improvement as well. Later on, the Actors' Committee presented statements of concern to the new Artistic Director, at one point requesting a seat on the Board of Governors. The group monitored and made formal requests about training, marketing, hirings, budgeting, ACTRA regulations, and other working conditions.[53] Assuming that these were not rubber-stamp entities (and the committee proceedings belie that notion), the feeling of investing in the company long-term via committee structures is something rarely found in commercial theater.

Nicholas also took it upon himself to create an award called The Nicholas Pennell Workshop Fund (beginning with a personal donation) in 1986. He had been at the University of Michigan teaching when French mime artist Marcel Marceau was invited in for workshops with the students. He discovered that Marceau would be interested in working with the Stratford company, but was embarrassed to discover that no budget money was available to pay the artist. He emphasized in a press release that visits from outsiders in special fields of expertise were even more important for a company with a long season in a distant location. It was completely in character for him to take the initiative and find a solution to providing ongoing training and stimulation for the corps of the company.

In 1994 when Richard Monette, another young rebel, took on the mantle of the directorship, he recalled that he had earlier been one of the critics of the Board of Governors and had even risen at a meeting to call them pigs. When he was invested into the artistic directorship, he wittily added that he now found himself at the trough. No doubt Nicky chuckled at this remark. Nonetheless, Pennell articulated very strong convictions in an interview in 1989:

> I am a child of the sixties. That was the period of my early adulthood. One thing that I realized was that politicians were either criminally stupid or criminally cynical.... There are very few exceptions to that rule....Going through the plays of Shakespeare that are politically motivated, one can see that things [remain] absolutely the same. They are still either criminally stupid or criminally cynical.[54]

In 1993, on *Desert Island Disks* he again spoke of the Stratford Festival's attempted recovery from the recession of the late 1980s and the fact that the government had frozen its support monies for arts institutions:

> ... The cultural industries in Canada, anyway, are responsible for 2% of the employment, and the money they bring into the economy is immense.... I'm bitter and extremely angry with the politicians in Canada because of their refusal to recognize the fact that the cultural industries are of great, great importance. Unless they are supported, we

shall be the poorer spiritually let alone financially… It's time to address [the problem] and to look at it squarely. I think that food should be on the table and that medical care should be available—but I also think it's essential that spiritual food is on people's tables. Otherwise, we will lose our cultural identity!

When Nicky found a soap-box available, he mounted it and let fly with reasoned and impassioned views. He spoke out on the radio and in newspaper interviews. Also, he was "on the road" a good bit of the time—performing, constantly fund-raising for the Festival, and stumping for the arts. This is one of the qualities that made him so attractive. He took Canadian citizenship—and then he took it seriously.

V.
Speak The Speech, I Pray You

VERY EARLY ON, NICKY FELT THE OBLIGATION to pass on what he knew about acting. In the 1970s, theater training schools had just gotten off the ground in Canada. Large numbers had already been established in the United States, branching out into universities where the training was dictated not by theater professionals but by professors of theater. The idea of apprenticeship was not promoted inside this schema for obvious reasons: 1) the professor could be at odds with the professional actor vis-a-vis training methodologies, 2) the professor of acting often did not have much experience in professional settings, and 3) the expert (the actor) did not possess the requisite university degrees nor conform to academic criteria. At the Festival itself, such rivalries did not occur.

Pennell saw the importance of creating opportunities for the apprentice actor in Canada. He and Marti Maraden and John Wood had performed scenes from *King Lear* for a touring show, and the intensive rehearsals were useful. Lear was a role Nicky always intended to play. How, he thought, are young actors going to have that same opportunity, to "have a bash" at the big roles:

Unless you have an adventurous director, you're not going to get your chance... at the big ones early so you have your ammunition going for you to do them later.[55]...Now beginning to happen at Stratford [is] that younger actors with perhaps less experience than needed for the part are getting to play [them]... in five or ten years' time that will pay off in spades when they come to them again or come to the bigger ones. .

The opening of a theater school at the Festival had been dangled as a possibility again and again, and Nicky was very much in favor of it, especially since his experience with the Young Company, a younger group of actors-in-training amassed by Robin Phillips who performed their own show every season, often with mentors like Nicky. The experience had been immensely rewarding. He lamented the fact that there were only a handful of the older generation of Canadian actors to go out and teach their craft to the younger ones. The beginning of the 1980s saw the first generation of actors coming out of the National Theatre School to build up that middle range of performers so important to repertory theater. Canada would feel that baby boom in the next four or five years and then it would be an exciting time, he said.

Thus, the notion of passing the torch was important, especially in his adopted country:

> The only way we tend to live on as an actor is in what we transmit to an audience, but more importantly, what we transmit to... young actors we work with. The whole idea that you pass on what experience you have—in my own case, people like Edith Evans, Laurence Olivier, Judi Dench, Maggie Smith, an extraordinary range of actors—-whatever I have gained... to enable the

generation behind you by your experience. To say "it's easier than that—-simply let go and you can fly."[56]

There is a constant kind of media pressure that says why can't we have stars in Stratford... I believe that unless we [properly train] our own generation, we will go on with the history of importing....I see the immense importance of bringing young people on.[57]

When I first came here [in 1972] 30-35% of the company was not Canadian. Now [in 1979] 7-10% of the company are not Canadian. I think that's marvelous... . [It's] one of the things that a lot of people overlook—said the Big Britisher![58]

Nicky's good friend and colleague John Broome, the movement coach at Stratford, described Nicky's global attitude about training:

> ...I most particularly remember what a wonderful company leader [Nicky] was. That was his strongest forte offstage was that he was determined never to let the side down. Many of the older actors and elder statesman performers felt that things like warm-ups and voice and body classes were things of the past to them—this was a stage they had passed through years ago and it wasn't necessary to continue with those now that they were fully fledged....But Nicky was different. He felt that he must set an example for the younger members of the company by being there himself, an admirable attitude.
>
> The old Medieval idea of the master and the apprentice, it's not different from that at all. You work with somebody who has got the experience

and the know-how and from that you develop confidence and knowledge and skill.[59]

In 1974, a pleasant change occurred in Nicky's life. He was discovered by a unique group of people whose tastes and interests coincided productively with his own. A surge of creative energy came from it, and the association was probably the basis for a number of the one-man shows he put together:

> [I found] a new kind of career that had never happened to me before. I was invited by the then Head of the Theater Department at The University of Michigan to be an artist in residence. That's something which now takes up my winters, working and spending time with students. I'm not a teacher, I'm an actor. But I work with them. Really my job is to be a kind of revolutionary, to get in under the academic and to say, forget all that. It's totally unimportant to you as an actor. It's instinct, instinct, instinct—don't rely on intellect. Which is an interesting job to do with people of that age.[60]
>
> The most difficult thing for a student in a professional theater training program is that they have to learn a lot of things. There have to be some givens, there have to be some theories handed to them, because they need a base on which to build.... [However] the only way they'll become actors is to take that as groundwork and throw it all away.... How important it is to remove everything that comes between you and the text. How important it is not be told something by an editor, or by a director, or by a book about the text. Not to accept that as truth.[61]

He had the heretical idea that student performances should simply not be released to the general public for viewing until both the cast and the director decided the production had reached a level of skill that made it ready for exposure: "Student productions are about process, not performance."[62] In fact, Nicky was never to lose his iconoclasm about actor training:

> . . . While it is virtually impossible to teach someone how to act—I mean, you cannot do it—whatever teaching there is to be done, should be done by people who are working within the theatre. I don't think that it should be a totally academic thing....
> The only way that one will have a really solid theatre is to have young actors who go through a period of training which you cannot get in drama school, you cannot get in universities... .[63]

The Head of the theater department at The University of Michigan was Dr. William P. "Doc" Halstead, also one of the early founders of the American Educational Theater Association (now called Association for Theater in Higher Education). Halstead was married to a diminutive dynamo known as "Claribel" (behind her back) and "Professor Baird" to her face. She knew Shakespeare like no one else, and once performed on a whim in New York; she was cited by Walter Kerr that year as the brightest newcomer in town.

It would be impossible to say whose ideas influenced whom, but Halstead and Baird were so significant in developing the world of educational theater and so much a part of the Michigan tradition of education that a more fortuitous aggregate of energies cannot be imagined. The University of Michigan was one of the great free-thinking universities. Only the best students were accepted.

Undergraduates had to have a 3.0 grade average or higher to enter the university, and graduate students needed a 3.25 or higher to enter graduate school. Guest artists and lecturers were brought in to enrich the education of the students on a regular basis. James Earl Jones taught workshops in the theater department, and people of the caliber of Helen Hayes were guests. The department also had a professional theater training program for graduate students. Pennell was treated like a master teacher and his intense interest in poets like Shakespeare, Eliot, and Lorca was mined for all the nuggets he had. Any maverick opinions he held were thoroughly encouraged.

In fact, when I first sought to interview Nicky in 1994, he had only one question for me, "Are you one of Claribel's kids?" The correct answer gave me an entree to everything he had to share about performance, and much of it was very familiar.

He performed the lead in *Pericles* and *Richard III* there and also directed *Oh, What a Lovely War!* and *As You Like It* with students.

The University of Michigan was Nicky's favorite of the residencies—indeed, he thought of it as "my time at university" since he'd not gone to college. He subsequently taught at Eastern Michigan University, another college nearby. Colleagues (who were graduate students with me at the University of Michigan at that time) Annette Martin and Dennis Beagen were at Eastern Michigan University, and both helped to arrange Nicky's guest residencies there. Nicky accepted invitations to teach at Northwestern University, Northern Michigan University, McMaster University, Windsor University, and a variety of other colleges for master classes and residencies. Nicky advised students to first go to university "to learn how to read"—by which he meant, to study and analyze text, to do critical reading—and once that had been achieved, to go on to professional theater school.

Teaching during the "off-seasons" (during the interim between the end of the Festival's repertory season in November and the beginning of the new year's rehearsals in February) was a unique choice. Most actors at Stratford opted to sign on for short-term acting jobs in other theaters around Canada. Nicky never classified himself as a teacher, yet he had a natural vocation for it. In his private papers were a large number of student letters that began, "You won't remember me, but I did a workshop (or a class, or a production) with you in 1978 and you said so many things that I will never forget..." at which point, the writer would add three pages of catching Nicky up on his/her recent achievements in theater work. There would be hand-made thank-you cards with lists of names and comments from students like "You changed my life," "I've never had an experience like this before," and "I've learned more this semester than I have in my entire life." He was clearly a skilled and much beloved mentor and role model. It is no wonder that he returned again and again for the rewards of all this animation and fire.

When Nicky's first official forays into directing happened in university settings, he commented:

> I've started to do some directing, not with any distinction, but I think I can explain from the actor's viewpoint what works better, what is dramatically viable, and what isn't. One of the hardest things to do as a director is... not to want other actors to give your performance.... You come in with certain ideas about the play, and then suddenly the actors' personalities begin to insist on a direction that is different from the one you originally thought. You have to have the courage and the ability to acknowledge and encourage their direction as right.[64]

Actor Stephen Ouimette, who has acted for a decade with the Stratford Festival, was one of those who had Nicky as a mentor:

> When I first worked at Stratford in 1979, Nicholas and Patricia Conolly and I did a version of *Pleasure and Repentance* at McMaster University. Just being in that show (aside from the fact that I was a young member of the company and getting to work with them) and learning by experience and listening and example was so necessary. I got to be there, to soak up what they were doing, then to try it on my own. They were very generous and gentle in that whole process. I learned a ton.
>
> Nicky and I taught a course in tandem to a summer program of 100 high school students. We did voice and movement, improvisation, and scenes. To this day, those students return to tell me how much they learned from Nicky.

Ouimette was allowed into Nicky's inner world and given the secrets of the craft:

> He loved to talk about the work. I was so like a sponge, just wanting to soak up any bit of information. Some of the things that he gave me I still go back to. Not always rules and techniques of acting but the reasons why you do it.
>
> He offered fantastic gifts, not the least of which was his unfailing courage to believe what he believed without apologizing to anyone. That is the little home fire that you keep burning in yourself, that keeps you going back. Being in this business is not easy. You have to keep that fire alight and he showed me how.

He gave me a lot of books—some of Edith Sitwell's poetry, the E.F. Benson *Lucia* series, and wonderful children's poetry.

But best of all, he gave me something that explains to me what it means to be an actor. It's from Eliot's *Four Quartets* in "East Coker," something which fuels my art:

There is, it seems to us
At best, only a limited value
    in the knowledge derived from experience.
The knowledge imposes a pattern and falsifies,
The pattern is new in every moment
And every moment is a new and shocking
Valuation of what we have been. We are only
    undeceived
By that which, deceiving, would no longer harm.
In the middle, not only in the middle of the way
But all the way, in a dark wood, in a bramble,
On the edge of a grimpen, where there is no
    secure foothold.
And menaced by monsters, fancy lights,
Risking enchantment. Do not let me hear
Of the wisdom of old men,
    but rather of their folly,
Their fear of fear and frenzy, their fear of
    possession
Of belonging to another, or to others,
    or to God.
The only wisdom we can hope to acquire
Is the wisdom of humility: humility is endless.

I always go back to that—there is no secure foothold, you are menaced by monsters and fancy lights, risking enchantment.

Ouimette emphasized that Nicky was a good teacher not so much in saying how you must do a thing but in encouraging you to find it yourself:

> Anytime he could inspire somebody to get something going—that was Nicholas. His love and care of the craft of acting. His willingness, not only that, his almost desperate need to continue it, to see it flourish, to see it grow and develop.

Ouimette added, "You know, he had names for everyone. He called me 'Snitch.' Hey, that's me. I'm snitching on him now."

In a very particular case, Nicky's mentoring turned into an enormously productive working relationship. The result was a performance mode that Nicky was to repeat again and again, often in the context of educational or outreach situations. Nicky carried out so many public relations tours for the Festival that he was specially recognized for it by John Hirsch.

In 1974, a petite and talented actor named Marti Maraden auditioned for Jean Gascon for the Festival. Although she'd done other professional work in the United States and Canada prior to her audition, she was given some smaller starter roles by Gascon, and "after three weeks of sheer terror," Nicky was the first to notice her and offer instruction in classical drama. He directed Tennessee Williams' *This Property is Condemned,* and it was in that production that she was showcased. She was subsequently offered leading roles at the Festival: "So Nicholas was incredibly important in helping me come forward and getting me ensconced in the company."[65]

Nicky then set about initiating a series of teaching-cum-performance opportunities. Since he had already spent a couple of off-seasons at The University of Michigan, he asked

Maraden if she would be his partner in some revenue-producing "two-handers," a shorthand term for an evening of performed entertainment for two actors that had minimal staging and neutral costuming, such as black costumes or black-and-white semi-formal dress. Of course, there were also one-handers (solo work), and three- and four-handers, occasionally called concert theater, chamber theater, drama quartets, readers theater, etc. The content and the format of these varied widely, but they were usually carried out by professional actors for a limited run, not longer than a week.

The original purpose was to help finance the teaching gigs Nicky, later adding Marti, intended to do. The duo offered a certain number of classes and workshops plus an evening or two of entertainment for a set salary. Each university took revenues from the public performances given. This was a convenient arrangement and usually quite appealing because the cost of hiring the performers was defrayed. The plan worked especially with universities that were out-of-the-way geographically and not near the nation's theater centers: It brought in needed instruction and professional role models for the students. These projects became more popular in the 1960s through the 1980s, but initiating the enterprise out of the Festival was unique and demonstrated Nicky's entrepreneurial bent. Robin Phillips (who occasionally directed the actors, which I suspect, means he looked over the work Nicky and Marti had already done for themselves) allowed them to say in the programme that the performers were traveling "under the auspices" of the Stratford Festival. So, the Festival did not contribute financial support but did offer costumes, props, some direction, and helpful critique.

The major part of this collaboration happened in 1977, 1978, and 1979. Maraden handled the bookings and travel arrangements, no mean task in terms of administration. It was clear from the letters sent that this was an educational endeavor as well as a show. Since the performers were salaried, the workshops and seminars were free to students. The acting workshops included warm-ups and voice skills but focused on text and scene study, with special attention to the problems of acting Shakespeare. The actors would also advise on directing projects in progress, and would participate in general question-and-answer sessions.

Maraden estimated that the two of them reached literally hundreds of actors. The 1977 tour included the University Theatre in Calgary; Muskingham College in Ohio; Monckton, St. John and Frederickton in New Brunswick; the University of Michigan; the Vancouver Playhouse; Wayne State University in Detroit; the Actors' Theater, Louisville; Groton School in Massachusetts; and Wright State University in Dayton, Ohio. The 1978 tour included a cruise on the Cunard line; Northwestern University; Loyola University; the University of Wisconsin, Milwaukee; Moorhead State College, Minnesota. 1979 saw them at Kent State in Ohio, several locations in Venezuela, and the Bermuda Arts Festival in Bermuda. A professor at Northwestern wrote an extended critique, all overwhelmingly favorable, "high-caliber and sustained inspiration." He emphasized how generous the actors were in the face of an overscheduled engagement, and that they were shared [66]among departments of theater, English and interpretation.[67] What had begun as a kernel of an idea took off and was so successful that they were invited for a number of return engagements. In fact, at the Bermuda Arts Festival, their colleague in performance was Victor Borge, who saw their performances and generously gave them a plug during his own.

Considering that these performances were carried out during the off-seasons, here were two very busy actors. After a time, they were joined by actor Tom Wood and Stage Manager Martin Bragg. For the most part, they performed a script devised by Michael Meyer, best known for his adaptations of Ibsen plays, called *Rogues and Vagabonds*. The focus of the performance was a literary and dramatic history of the profession of acting, beginning with the denunciations of Elizabethan politicians and clergymen, who ranked actors along with thieves and whores, and advancing through to the first actor awarded a knighthood, Sir Henry Irving at the end of the nineteenth century. The program sought to convey an impression of the actor as an artist and included works from Shakespeare, Wilde, Congreve, and also commentary and witty snippets from Samuel Johnson, Charlotte Bronte, Charles Dickens, Noel Coward, and Ogden Nash.

It is a credit to the duo that the shows were often reviewed by sophisticated theater critics. One described the evening as "ablaze with the cadences of great literature... memories of a noble professional nobly involved with the art of the theater." He added:

> Mr. Pennell took one of the greatest risks I've yet seen an actor dare in a theater.... This was in a piece about Edmund Kean, about whom Coleridge said, "was like reading Shakespeare by flashes of lightning." Then Pennell began talking about Kean's last appearance, at the age of 44. Kean was playing Othello, with his son as Iago, and death slowly overtook him during the performance... . Suddenly Pennell himself was playing Kean performing Othello at this moment of Kean's final glory and ultimate defeat. No actor could be quite sane and undertake so difficult a feat. But Pennell, in rather casual contemporary dress and without the benefit of scene trappings, pulled off the trick with stunning theatricality.[68]

A radio critic paid tribute to Maraden at a performance in the Fall of 1977, "for whom this performance marked her triumphant—and we don't use the world lightly—her triumphant return to a Vancouver stage where she is so fondly remembered." The reviewer gave tribute to the entire Festival:

> Not surprisingly, these are the qualities that distinguish the "Phillips Style" of acting as it has emerged over the past few seasons at Stratford: an uncluttered and spare yet rich and eloquent style that speaks directly and simultaneously to both heart and head, and leaves the hearer invigorated yet clear-headed, as if after spending two hours drinking in the view from some high, but not remote, mountain peak.... Nicholas Pennell's ability to rivet with a simple anecdote, or to bring an excerpt from Dickens' *Nicholas Nickleby* leaping off the page, or to evoke the shades of great actors of the past like Kean and Irving. Here is an actor for whom we have the greatest respect for the power and subtlety of his voice and carriage and gesture, the razor-edge of balanced control along which he moves his performance....

There was more:

> Their performances are intimately connected with an unbroken stage tradition going right back to Shakespeare and before—yet never fusty or hidebound. Indeed, they are breathtakingly, exhilaratingly contemporary—yet never modish or trendy. These are truly classic performances... . If the generation after Gielgud and Olivier is to discover its natural and appropriate stage style, Maraden and Pennell are pointing the way to what that style can and should be at its best.[69]

At a certain point, Marti and Nicky talked about adding a script to their repertoire. The title was *This Fair Child of Mine* and the motif was an exploration of the relationships of parents and children in scenes from Shakespeare. Maraden did the bulk of the groundwork and research, and Nicky did the all-important structuring of the work. They collaborated on scene selection, balance, and the division of actual lines. This script was considerably heftier than *Rogues and Vagabonds* and had clearly gone through a number of reincarnations as the original script would probably have run over three hours. *Rogues and Vagabonds* played at about two hours, which shows how engaging these performers were. Such scripts are best clocked in at slightly over one hour. There is no record of how often *This Fair Child of Mine* was performed.

In the early 1980s, Nicky compiled an anthology performance called *Wooing, Wedding, and Repenting*, which was performed a couple of times and then became the kernel of a later version, further adapted by Elliott Hayes, called *A Variable Passion*. The latter work used a compilation of light and dark, long and short selections about love, courtship, and the joys and drawbacks of marriage, all woven into a dramatic conceit: A professor of literature has been unfaithful and his wife has terminated their relationship; he dons his clothes, cleans the flat, calls her, but they do not reconcile. The script was performed on a set which had a desk, bookshelves and a daybed. The performance was so successful it was invited to be part of the festival season in 1982. It was performed in Chicago and several places in the United States and Canada. There is a videotape of a performance of this script in the Stratford Archives.

Nicky performed a number of short entertainments throughout his career, such as reading from the work of John Betjeman in Detroit in 1976; performing T.S. Eliot's *Four Quartets* with Maraden in 1979; performing *The Rose and the*

Fire, selections from Lorca with guitarist Liona Boyd in Chicago at the Art Institute in 1972; *Nine Lessons and Carols* for CBC in 1982; performance of *That Shakespeare Rag*, compiled by Elliot Hayes, for the Shakespeare Association of America in 1986; narration for Christmas and other special events readings.

All of the scripts demonstrated a mastery of difficult literature, a ready command of performance technique, and alternated between direct connection with an audience and the closed scene. The large number of invitations tells us he was known as an actor of acute intelligence and versatility.

There is occasional wonderment about why Nicky didn't eventually turn to full-time directing. The idea is speculative, of course, as if directing were a higher art form, somehow privileged over acting. Acting is a fulfilling profession, complete unto itself, which Nicholas chose to complement at times with another honorable profession, teaching. There is no mystery here but an act of preference. Nicky directed about half a dozen theater pieces, but he never prioritized that work. One newspaper article revealed, "He believes his future will be in directing, but he isn't rushing to it. 'Directing is fine, he said, 'but it takes you out of acting and you're done when the fun begins.'"[70]

Others wonder why Nicky never sought roles in Canadian theater during the off-seasons. He explained to me that he took the jobs he was invited to do. There is the possibility that he had certain misgivings regarding what nationalists might feel about his competing for roles they thought were theirs — he was certainly sensitive to the dilemma. His English accent, of course, would continue to advertise that he was invading Canadian turf.

VI.
Advice To The Players

AN ACTOR WHO HAS ALSO TAUGHT ACTING tends to be very articulate because he has developed ways to speak to novices: Nicky spent 34 years as an actor and was teaching during at least 21 of them. The interview tapes and written material about him demonstrate a strong consistency in his opinions about acting the craft. He'd clearly developed a pedagogical repertoire.

This chapter contains an overview of Nicky's ideas about the performance of Shakespeare, describes what means he used to achieve characterization, delineates details about voice and diction and other aspects of technique, and briefly discusses audiences and critics. My extended interview of Nicky in 1994 focused exclusively on the subject of theater, so he provided several topics as well as the direction of his thinking about performance. Ordinarily, he would have read this book and have made adjustments prior to its publication; regrettably, that is no longer possible.

Nicky's philosophy of theater was a subject he warmed to and had obviously debated over the years, not only with other actors and directors but in his public interviews. He had settled on certain qualities of theater as more engrossing and more resonant than others. He told Ivor Novello: "I don't think it's a good thing to make people feel that eased and that relaxed.... people ought to feel threatened by theater. I never think they ought to feel comfortable." He said the same in an interview with Susan Smith: "It should be something that. . .makes uncertain because only in an atmosphere of uncertainty will you start to think. When you are comfortable and secure, you won't–it's safer not to, you know."

Although theater should delight, Nicky felt that theater should be intellectually engaging as well, forcing the auditor to consider and weigh. He thought that modern directors should locate contemporary images which reflect what the script is saying. He accepted what Robin Phillips had to say about this, yet it was clear that the topic of "relevance" had been argued over and cogitated. For Nicky, relevance did not mean actors making their own political statements—which would blinker them and shut down their creative stimuli—but that a production, even of Shakespeare, should have a correspondence with issues in contemporary life.

Relevance is one of the war cries of directors of the late twentieth century. It was Sir Peter Hall's primary ideology—making Shakespeare modern—when he took over the Royal Shakespeare Company in 1958. Robin Phillips recalled his early trips to Stratford in 1973 when he was being considered for the position of Artistic Director: "[The Festival] didn't seem terribly in touch. It was like going down a country road, turning a corner, and finding a Ruritanian something." Phillips looked for the relationship between the citizens of Canada and the theater at Stratford: "I couldn't see any human connection." A disconnect was echoed in the acting style, especially in classical drama, as if "period people were not real, that they were painted dolls running around."[71]

Nicky knew the truth of these observations. He did not feel that theater should be fantasy (a risky word for theater, dangerously close to frivolous) but rather a necessary escape, a willing suspension into an alternate reality, important to relieving us of "the absolute mundane-ness of the 9-to-5 kind of life."[72]

Nicholas Pennell was one of the major textualist actors working. Nicholas Rudall, one of Nicky's directors at the Court Theater in Chicago, said that he always pronounced it "TEK-ST—like that—indicating that it had some sort of divine property that you could not omit."[73] Words, words, words were always the fulcrum of Pennell's way of working. His major strategy was to read the text again and again, over and over. Another of his directors, Michael Halberstam at the Writers' Theater, declared,

> Nicholas was a method actor because he gave that depth of emotion. But he did not come up with that until he completely owned the text, was going in the text's direction, until he'd mined it and knew everything it had to offer.[74]

The text was a score and a blueprint. However, that did not mean that the text was a magic clue to every actor who would, once s\he has unlocked it, find "the only way" or "the right way" to speak that text. The text was a stimulus to discovering a universal center in the character's truth and then to creating the details in the actor's own light, in the context of his own raw materials as an artist, his own experience, his own emotional capacities, his own personal equipment, his own way of manifesting actions and reactions to the language.

What was Nicholas looking for in text? Several fundamentals emerge. First of all, he would tease a poetic/dramatic image to death, pronouncing the word over and over again, relishing and locating its sound in his own body. So it began to filter through his experiential screen. When teaching, he said that every word had three levels of meaning: first, its literal or dictionary meaning; secondly, one's personal memory or internal emotional vision of the word; and, finally, the "mantra meaning" where one's internal self expresses its taste or essence. All of these are used by the actor to stimulate a personalized response to the word even though, eventually, there may be too much information to process and only one meaning could be selected to convey in performance. This was particularly true of Shakespeare, where the performer was attempting to communicate the complexity of 400-year-old language.

Nicky also sought out what was for him a major device of poetry, anthesis. He was interested not just in labeling the literary tool but in trying to convey it vocally. It was usually manifest in balanced sentences which were putting two different words or two different ideas into opposition. This, in turn, dictated using the voice in such a way as to show the antithetical meanings, which might mean leaving the voice "up" or unresolved on the first idea emphasized, and then bringing it down into resolution for the second idea emphasized.

Antithesis is a major structural feature of Shakespeare's plays, and discovering the psychological and group meanings of language helps the audience by showing that words have color and sounds related to meaning. Inflecting words for an audience demonstrates their importance in a line of dialogue and in the scheme of the play. This latter is also called emphasis, showing actors how to correctly feature, enhance, or de-emphasize a word or a particular phrase. For example, Beatrice must say to Benedick, "You have stayed me in a happy *hour*" rather than "You have stayed me in a *happy* hour," in IV.i.284 of *Much Ado About Nothing* (so that they will not seem to be discussing drinking in a bar.)

The text was open to orchestration by the actor. The actor should not rewrite the notes of score, but he could feel very free about punctuating it, which relates essentially to inserting it, an actor's chief task. Firmly built into his philosophy was the requisite that acting is a creative art: Just as a violinist or a singer has the right to offer an interpretation of a musical piece, an actor needs to bring his own artistry and emotional storehouse to Shakespeare's language.

For many years, Nicky used to "wite-out" (block it out with a liquid correction fluid) the punctuation before he went to work on the text. He did not do this in an effort to obliterate what Shakespeare wrote but rather to obliterate what others had imposed onto Shakespeare. Nicky had studied the history of Shakespeare's texts and had listened to those who espoused using the punctuation of the earliest texts (Quartos and early Folios); ultimately, he felt that it was virtually impossible to locate the punctuation that Shakespeare personally had intended or even used. So many compositors, printers, and editors intervened between Shakespeare and the text that the actor was being dangerously misled. Much of the punctuation was added or tampered with after Shakespeare's death by people who were editing for readers, not for performance. This contamination of the text included:

> Those Samuel French acting editions, where you tend to get the stage manager's view of the production, rarely do you get the actor's — or those terrible little stage directions in brackets — [sneers], [laughingly] — that tell you how to play it. So all I have left after I have used the 'wite-out' is text, and I go by that."[75]

He believed passionately that the actor needed to completely own the text in order to enliven it, that the plays were not literary objects but were primarily written to be performed. Given the amount of scholarship on this subject accumulated by the twenty-first century, one would think this statement would be a cliché and universally believed. Not so:

> As much as I respect a lot of Shakespeare scholars, my grave problem is the fact that the man wrote so that he would be performed. He wrote for an

audience that was 50-60% illiterate, could not read or write, so these words were created for an audience who could only receive via the spoken word.... When you realize that Shakespeare wrote in order to be performed, not to be studied and analyzed, you have to change your judgements quite a lot.... To fathom Shakespeare is really not very difficult if you see a good production of it. The point is that the play will have different secrets for other people at other times. Why he is the greatest playwright is because he goes on being available and fathomable to generation after generation, on varying levels for each auditor. Again, it is taking the rose apart to find the scent. This is true in a lot of artistic endeavor. I've very often had to say to a director [as we were rehearsing], "Please don't say anything about that.... It's happening organically, and if you tell me it's good, I'll start trying to dolly it up.... The really really good directors rarely tell you when you are being good. They'll tell you when you're being bad, and the rest they'll take on trust [because] they know you're on the right track.[76]

The subject of characterizing, creating a role, was raised in every single session Nicky had with students; in fact, one reporter picked up on the answer in a newspaper article entitled, "You create the role out of yourself, says Pennell."[77] The question grows out of a time-honored debate in acting schools over whether or not the "true" actor is one who plays himself each time—as, say, Cary Grant or Spencer Tracy appeared to—or whether it was better for the actor to become an entirely different character, one almost not recognizable onstage. Clearly the premise has several arguable sub-issues, and Nicky cut through it by saying:

> You cannot become someone else onstage: You can
> only be yourself. You elevate the characteristics
> and the emotional and imaginative experiences
> of your own that parallel the character's. It is the
> bit of you that is Hamlet or King John that you
> pump up or heighten. There are also qualities you
> have to suppress—no, that's the wrong word—
> there are bits you have to minimize.

Having said this, it was clear that Nicky could achieve that technique, and the result was that he would almost totally obscure himself in a character. When I was watching *Cyrano de Bergerac* (with Colm Feore as Cyrano in 1994), I was aware that at a certain point, someone had entered, back to the audience at the rear of the stage. It was a very strong, authoritative presence and I began to wish he would turn around. Once he did, a threatening element had clearly invaded the scene, and another of the power centers of the play had been established. About five minutes later, it hit me that this was the man I'd interviewed a few days before, this was Nicholas Pennell playing Comte de Guiche. The same thing happened on the night he played small roles in a Molière double-bill. I'd read the program first this time, and kept waiting for Pennell to enter—to my surprise, he had already gotten himself onstage and was unrecognizable in a peasant costume.

A number of actors at the Festival cite the maxim of creating from your own inner resources as one of the greatest gifts Robin Phillips ever gave. When Phillips arrived as Artistic Director, he was alarmed by "seeing all these gifted young actors, yet so many of them had this idea of copying whatever they encountered in other performances."[78] This was not apprenticing, not mentoring, but merely imitating. Phillips used very personalized devices to force an actor to deliver a truthful and fresh performance, saying "Anything is permissible if it will produce something more real and true from the actors involved."[79] Both William Hutt and Brian Bedford opined that they were able to develop their own sense of a character, their own style of classical acting, their own signature styles of acting under Phillips' tutelage. Marti Maraden stated that Phillips' philosophy extended to every actor onstage:

> In a crowd scene, he had the gift of making each person feel he was a living, breathing human being. He spent extraordinary amounts of time working out tiny bits of character business for each actor. He was always worrying that people in a crowd tended to lose their identity.

I asked Nicky if he did research, extensive reading of critics, theater reviews, or video-viewing about the role or about the play. In Shakespeare, especially, characters are written about by a great many scholars but only rarely by actors. He did not side-step the question, but his answer indicated that he depended much more on the Stanislavskian tenet of observation and that, for him, was his own kind of research.

Nicky had been a bit stung by research early in his acting career so was wary of its influence. He had read a book scholars had been enchanted by—Ernest Jones' *Oedipus and Hamlet*—as he was preparing to play Hamlet in 1976. He told fellow actor Richard Monette, with whom he was sharing the role, that he was very taken with this idea that Hamlet wanted to supplant his father in his mother's bed. Two weeks before the show opened, Nicky changed his mind completely and told Monette he'd re-thought the interpretation and decided to chuck it, whereupon Monette told him it hadn't worked for Olivier either! Despite this experience, one Nicky would tell and retell, he was a great reader and he couldn't bypass some form of research altogether. He was too interested in literature and the people who created it.

His observation tactics included watching people, how they walk, talk, dress, move, behave and live their lives. This material filtered into the actor's subconscious (because after years of doing it, even the paying attention to life became subliminal). Once when he was in rehearsal to play Iago, his director noted that she liked the Manchester accent he was using. He was astounded and asked her what she meant. He realized then that an NCO from the Army during his year in the National Service had begun to emerge—"had crawled out"—as the villain, complete with the remembered speech patterns.

Nicky also avidly read the newspapers and listened to radio news and found that certain contemporary images had correspondences or parallels within the text of the plays he was working on. Any biography, poetry, or sources of his general reading might present him with emblems of the character. But he never consciously patterned himself on a specific model or person or animal or anything like that, because he felt he would then be doing a bad imitation. When he was working on the character of Siegfried Sassoon for *Not About Heroes*, Nicky read Sassoon's poetry and, of course, the text of the play. Although this is clearly what most dramaturgs mean by research, Nicky saw such study as *de rigeur*.

Nicholas Rudall told an interesting story about Nicky playing Henry Higgins in Shaw's *Pygmalion* at the Court Theater:

> It was always a matter of his ability to do research. When we were rehearsing *Pygmalion*, I remember that Michael Holroyd's massive three-volume (600 pages each) work on Shaw had just come out. It was typical of the way we worked that both Nicky

and I read it. The first part is about Shaw's early life, in which the idea of a *ménage à trois* comes up because of Shaw's father being a drunkard, his mother having an affair with an artist, and Holroyd (without going too far with this) shows that every single Shaw play has an *a trois* relationship—*Arms and the Man, Devil's Disciple*, etc. Shaw's connection to his mother is a very complicated one, even so in *Pygmalion*. So, Shaw's relationship with his mother became the focus in [our production] where the mother did what (obviously) Shaw's mother did. Mrs. Higgins always says, "Sit down, Henry," and there are many lines in the play (from Higgins) about how if he were to marry someone, it would be someone like his mother. All this stuff resonating from the Holroyd biography was in Pennell's mind while we were working on the part.

So it was not just all text—it was also subtext of a profound kind....

During our interview, Nicky called the subject of research "vexed," and I think it was a caveat to himself that he should, as Rudall says earlier, reserve the right to reject what the research unearthed. Nearer the end of his life, he gave an interview to Diana Mady Kelly and Sue Martin in *Windsor Review*, which is worth re-printing in part:

WR: To create a character where do you begin?
Pennell: I read the text. I don't allow myself to intellectualize. Instinct and the subconscious will operate. If one would only trust the text! It works.

WR: Do you use a particular method to create a role? To analyze a role?

Pennell: No. Eclecticism. Scavenging. Use anything you can lay your hands on. Theories are meant to be shot down. To tell the truth is the only theory about acting.

WR: Do you form an image of the character you are going to play?
Pennell: Yes and no. More so since I've been playing wonderful eccentrics such as Ford [*The Merry Wives of Windsor*, 1982] and Jacques [1983]. You tend to form mental images as rehearsal progresses. However, you cannot become someone else. You can only play yourself. You always play a part of yourself. You cannot form an image that isn't part of you.

WR: Is costuming an important part in the development of the role?
Pennell: No. Desmond Heeley told me, "I don't want to design the costume until you develop the role."

WR: Do you look for the differences or similarities between yourself and your character, when you read a script?
Pennell: Never contradictions, only similarities. Bad acting is not observing similarities. Everything is observation.[80]

One of the reasons that Nicky's precise method will always be irretrievable is that language is exasperatingly inexact when one wants to describe mental processes, especially as they relate to acting. Also, actors, like critics or theorists or people who have been teachers, tend to use "you should" words, when what usually happens within the creative process of an artist is that some of it will be relevant to only that artist. A good artist creates a whole new system of entering the role, including imaginative touchstones and physical and mental processes appropriate to himself or herself. That is the definition of the job.

One has to devise a vocabulary from one's own experience with the art if one is inclined to teach it. Teachers of acting rarely say, "Here's how I do it. Take or leave what you find useful or effective." Furthermore, of course, is that an actor's personal method develops over the years—grows, thickens, accumulates, broadens, contracts, is pruned.

For Nicky, an important source of the actor's raw material was adapted from his reading about performance:

> The final thing would be what Genet calls "the wound." It is the ongoing well of experience from which you draw. The artist consistently doesn't allow scabs to form. His job is to pick away all the time at the edge of it to make sure that what he is drawing on is emotionally accurate and truthful. The imaginative life is not merely remembered, rather it's active—the pain, the joy. It's probably the most important source.

This idea sounds close to what Stanislavsky might have been after in describing "sense memory" and "emotion recall," although Nicky's description is much deeper and more interesting because it refers to a fund of collected emotional experiences such as highly sensitive and highly sensitized artists naturally imprint over time. Nicky made these comments to Kelly and Martin during his interview with them:

> I think a constant demand is made on the artist in life... . but the demand is that you never, never,

never put yourself through therapy, your own personal therapy. You must never allow scar tissue to form. And the wounds must be kept bleeding; you have to consistently pick around the edge of the scab so that your *emotional recall* [italics mine], both for grief and for joy, is absolutely accurate and truthful. The moment you allow an accretion of tissue over the scar you will start not recording it accurately. You will start recording a kind of watered-down, a kind of expurgated version of that experience, and the artist cannot do that.

What is the most difficult for the actor is that with acting, more than painting or writing, one is faced with the fact that a superb technique can mask completely, and an audience will never know there is nothing inside. Now you can't do that as an artist, a painter. You can't do that as a composer. People become aware of it. But as an actor, you can. One knows and has known actors who simply are brilliant technicians, and truly fool all of the people all of the time, but inside they must know, that it is not real....[81]

An enormously important resource for Nicky was his director. He'd had a remarkable experience with Jean Gascon in *Pericles*, where the director put the cast through extensive movement exercises and used large dance-like sequences during the transitions of scenes, and this helped free up Nicky physically, as well as made him permanently interested in movement training for performers.

Nicky had a special affinity for John Hirsch, who he said made him laugh: He knew Hirsch was sometimes too direct, too crudely honest, "but a very courageous man, a very funny man." Nonetheless, Nicky declared that he'd done his best work for Robin Phillips, whose approaches to acting provided an important secret of performance:

Robin I'd known for many years, we were both
young actors [they were both in a film of *David
Copperfield* as in *Forsyte Saga* together].... I was at
a point where it was perhaps a little easier for me
to open up. His method of working, the whole
improvisational area...was a great risk at that
time, but a very exciting one to take.[82]

Nicky admired Phillips exorbitantly and thought him an
astonishing teacher as well as director. Phillips influenced
him early on by denouncing "the semaphore thing," by which
he meant the excessive declaiming British classical actors did
with text.[83] Phillips described the constant lecturing and
speechifying as "deeply boring" and introduced the idea of
variety in vocalization, muttering and sighing and
whispering in addition to (and to replace) ranting and
shouting. He was equally exact about gesture: "I believe
earth-shattering emotions are tiny... . It's ridiculous to feel
you have to... spew emotion all over the stage.[84] *Toronto Star*
critic Urjo Kareda (who eventually became literary manager)
summed up:

People caught their breath to hear murmured
conversations [in Phillips' 1977 *Measure for
Measure*]. Flickers of emotion were caught from
faces which seemed suddenly intimately close.
Nuances were captured and held for lengths with
later details. The accumulation of tension hovered
over the action with electrifying intensity.[85]

Nicky offered more:

. . .The most valuable thing Robin did was to
constantly remind an actor that he must never
exceed the possiblities of reality.... Never expand

an emotional state beyond its reality in your own experience... you had to hold it at a point of personal reality.

People have called him a manipulative director because he does get in and deals with individuals' emotions. I would suggest that almost without exception all great artists do this in one way or another.... A lot of his power as a director is that he goes directly to the source of... your personal emotional energy, not a generalized thing. To *yours*... .

You sit there and hear him talking to another actor and you think, "Why don't you say that to me? I can do that quite easily!" Why he then says to you something that you think "I can't do that!" is because he is demanding something more of you individually.... He knows your weaknesses, he knows your strengths, and those are the things he's after. He'll wait, he's immensely patient. It's rather like a huntsman watching a rabbit hole. Robin will wait sometimes for weeks to see the tip of a pair of ears. He knows that the performance he wants may be tucked away someplace that the actor doesn't see. He induces by cajoling, very rarely by bullying—by insisting long past the point where you've said no he goes on insisting. In some magical way he gets you to do the kind of acting that literally nobody else could... . That's the greatest satisfaction.[86]

On a number of aspects of technique, Nicky was firm and disciplined. Like a dancer, he continually took classes for his body and his voice. The stage in the Stratford Festival Theatre is like no other in the world, specifically designed by Guthrie and Moisievitch to accommodate audience on three sides. A skilled actor can manipulate it wonderfully, and Nicky's determination to have the most flexible vocal instrument possible was part of his love for working in that space.

In 1984, voice coach Patsy Rodenburg came to Stratford and the two colleagues had very similar points of view, so much so that they learned from each other and stimulated one another:

> I'd come over from London to take over the voice department when Hirsch was the Artistic Director. Nicky was one of the first people in class. I'd known him from *The Forsyte Saga* but I'd had no idea he was such a brilliant classical actor (I worked with him on Oberon, but he did a remarkable Fool to Douglas Campbell's Lear in 1984.) He was in class every day and we worked together until he died.
>
> He was a craftsperson. He was from a generation of actors where the actor's craft [i.e.,technique] was so ingrained that it often stopped the spontaneity of the work. That was never the case with Nicky, actually—he did what every great actor did—he used craft. By 1984, a lot of the technical stuff he knew was being abandoned, was no longer part of the training. Although he used much of it, he also humanized it. He did this with every role he played. In the middle of the 1980s, there were a lot of directors who were very specific [as they directed], not necessarily allowing actors to make their own choices. Nicky managed to do everything a director wanted him to do and yet he would add his own qualities to the role.
>
> What I mean by a craftsperson is that one has to be doing that work every day. Nicky did his breathing exercises, his freeing exercises, he did

his range, his tone exercises, his articulation exercises—he never took anything for granted. He worked (god, he worked) with diligence. This led him into technical freedom. He could fill the Festival Theatre with his own voice because he had done all the groundwork.

How dare actors think they can go onstage and speak a great classical text without work! Nicky knew how to serve the text without reducing it to the casual. What he could do was get heightened but still be real. Heightened reality, I call it.

He was a fantastic role model for the others. He was always in class. He knew that as you speak Shakespeare, you speak yourself into consciousness, you transform, you move through something.[87]

Movement Coach John Broome recalled a day in his movement class:

I said, now everybody stand in a circle holding hands and just lifting the arms up and breathing in and letting them fall and breathing out. Then I said, now take it from Nicky, and let the breath out slowly. That was the worse thing I could have said because he'd got such phenomenal breath control. Nobody could keep up with him—they were all gasping for breath while he'd got oodles left.

Clifford Turner, a voice teacher at RADA, taught a method called "rib reserve," which meant that you drew breath into the rib cage and then breathed again, (without letting the first breath out) into the diaphragm. The first breath took care of most of the lines. What was left was a full ribcage of breath that was held in reserve just in case the actor needed to continue on through a very long extended thought. Although the technique was probably needed more for the old-fashioned declamatory style of speaking Shakespeare, it would, nevertheless, encourage larger intakes of breath before attacking a line. Nicky said that Turner improved the resonance and the scale of his voice so that when his voice matured in his early thirties, the whole resonating chamber became larger and more encompassing.

"Rib reserve" was one of those methods from drama school training that was abandoned in late twentiety-century voice training. Patsy Rodenburg explained that "rib reserve" required actors to hold their ribs up or elevated for long periods of time, a positioning that was not completely natural nor altogether good for the anatomy. She commented that "Nicky had a good chest and a good rib-swing, but we worked to free it up a bit," in order to allow him more relaxation in delivery. He had his routines, but "if something wasn't working and I'd say 'let's try something else,' he'd break all the molds. He had all that craft and all that tradition and yet he was so forward-looking."

Nicky's barrel-shaped chest was legendary, commented on by Desmond Heeley, who costumed him, and Marti Maraden as well, who directed him. She occasionally had to tone his volume down so that the other actors' voices would not be diminished by the strength and energy of Nick's.

Once asked what professional-school training provided for him, Nicky replied:

> Probably the most important is the intensive vocal and physical training.... [of what] Truman Capote once rather unkindly called "the smug baritone of the trained actor."...I thought that was a mean cut because in fact it's taken me a long time to even remotely have the kind of flexibility that I hope I have now. It took me ten years and I trained with very good people.[88]

Nicholas Rudall commented about pronunciation and projection regarding Nicky's vocalization:

> . . . Since he mainly acted in language plays, Shaw and Shakespeare, his ability to get his tongue around sound meant that he required of himself and everyone around him impeccable diction. He declared—if you're working in the theater and you can't hear what's being said around you, the management shouldn't be charging money.[89]

Nicky said that he was not particularly tied to metering-out of Shakespeare's iambic pentameter (i.e., counting the beats or iambs) nor did he believe in overly strict adherence to verse rules. He did feel that actors were helped by relearning the freedoms and the rhythms of childhood and emphasized "the whole thing of saying to students 'why fight verse?' because some [experts] believe that iambic pentameter is the [rhythm of the] heartbeat."[90] He certainly knew about meter and verse, knew what they meant in a passage, but found himself disinclined to worry if a foot was missing, "less wedded to absolute metrical accuracy as I get on." The pentameter gives support like a trampoline with a bounce along the top of the textual line, he claimed, and that was helpful in speaking it.

Patsy Rodenburg added to this rather casual analysis of Nicky's use of meter in classical verse:

> His knowledge of verse-speaking was remarkable. He took all the components of verse-speaking— iambic pentameter, line energy, and he humanized it. You didn't necessarily know he was being strictly correct, but he was always perfect [in observing the verse]. He was the sort of artist who could do all the fingering and yet add his soul.

He was one of those actors who had the language, the rhythm, the structure in his bloodstream: He had access to it without having even to think. What a great actor does all the time is to know the words so well that s/he forgets the text. Some of these were a bit dead emotionally, but not Nicky—he could finger the text, play it accurately, and still have a bedrock of emotion there. I don't mind an actor breaking the rules as long as s/he knows the rules. Great actors break rules—Nicky did so from the point of view of choice.

When asked by an interviewer if he went into the first rehearsal of each play with all his lines memorized, Nicky replied in the negative:

I think learning lines is a technical trick. I'm talking purely personally now. For me, it's exactly like typing. If you do a-s-d-f, you know, fingering [the typewriter keys], that is exactly the same as learning lines.... What is vitally important is something we call subtext which is the thought process that is going on underneath the lines when you speak them. The whole basis of the character, the whole foundation of the character, is in the subtext. It's where you go emotionally, what your feelings are, what your thoughts are, the whole arc of the play.

Now if that is clear to you, then the lines will come, or should come, really, as you rehearse. Basically if one's lucky enough to be rehearsing a play for over a month or six weeks (unless you have a director who demands lines in a short space of time), you'll find after a week or two weeks you begin to know them, and after three weeks, they go in without your having to sit down and ding-ding-ding-ding learn them…. Finally the marriage of the subtext and the text becomes such that no other words will do. You simply cannot express yourself by any other means. Because the connection—the emotional connection, the intellectual connection—is such that it throws off little roots into each word so that if you say, "O what a rogue and peasant slave am I," the word *rogue*, the word *peasant*, the word *slave*, the word *I*—all those things have a connection so rooted in yourself that only the text will serve you. In other words, you could not speak any other line.[91]

Movement coach John Broome talked about Nicholas' famous "Dover roll," a slight oscillation from side to side in his walk that Broome used to correct. Nicky loved that label because he would imagine the rotund farmers of Devon that he knew when he was a child.

One of the things Nicky had onstage was a powerful sense of the audience. He actually watched how Maggie Smith worked the audience as well, because her connection with them was legendary—to the point where, if someone coughed, she would automatically repeat the word that might have been obscured. Nicky described his connection with them as being like an antenna, always out there and rotating and picking up signals. His observations about that entity called audience come both from being on the stage and being in the audience:

. . . This is by no means an irreligious thing to say—[theater is] a form of transubstantiation. It's an ability to enter into a community revelation, and to actually allow yourself to be changed, to be transmuted…. It happens individually, of course… rarely have I experienced the total union, either as actor or as audience—it has happened once or twice but not very often. Time and time again, isolated units in that audience, someone, will allow themselves to go with it. And one is aware of that (somewhere subconsciously) in the back of one's mind, one knows it....The very great evenings in the theater are when... the actors, the text, the audience are so at one that it's a moment of absolute communion.... Where theater differs almost from any other is that it is a community experience.

You know, it's this ongoing belief that actors are rogues and vagabonds.... From the very earliest times [actors] were playing out other people's "alternate realities," if you like. There is something dangerous, risk-taking, in that.

Added to which is a great deal of hogwash... about theater and cinema as an escape from reality.... It is not an escape *from* but an escape *into*. I think it's a deliberate flight into another reality—in a book, in a picture, in a piece of music, in a theater, wherever it happens, but that seems to be good, not bad. The wonderful thing about schools audiences is that they're close enough... to their childhood to allow themselves to go with you. It's exciting because a lot of the time they reject it and they are very verbal about their rejection.[92]

Nicky was terribly conscious of the transitory nature of his art form:

There's an interesting thing about acting: actors exist in the moment.... They come, and they disappear when they go, their work is not remembered. Even if the work is recorded on TV or radio, that automatically places [it] into a different [medium].[93]

Even if you brought the same audience back in exactly the same conditions on exactly the same day with exactly the same weather, it still would not be the same [performance given].[94]

About the subject of newspaper critics, every actor has an opinion. Nicky was often asked if he read reviews. He replied carefully:

Late in the season. Because no matter how objective you try to be, they can be destructive. I remember one review where the critic said... that he could not understand why I'd been cast for the part at all (this was *Richard II*), that I was a spear-carrier promoted far beyond my talents in the theater, that I had neither the wit nor the intelligence to try the part. He undercut his statement...[because] I've never been a spear-carrier with this company or with any other company, so the sting went out of the insult. No matter how much [he] disliked my performance, [he'd] been inaccurate about it.

What can be destructive is what [the reviewer] omits....The reviews may persuade you you were wrong, persuade you to try to alter a performance, and that is wrong. Good notices can be equally dangerous and push the whole [production] too far.

It's the assumption that you've spent two months [in rehearsal] trying to get it wrong![95]

However, Nicky did offer a solution to what most actors consider a necessary evil:

> I think it would be very easy to dismiss critics and I think this would be wrong.... Yet, [an actor] has to be very careful of [critical] judgements that are ill-informed. I don't think it's possible to judge anyone's performance unless you judge it in the light of their previous work, over a period of several years.... I think there is a lack of desire to do homework, the knowledge that backs up the critical faculty. When I think of the work of [London critics like] Bryden, Tynan, Hobson— these people who have painstakingly built up years of experience with theater, who will go miles to discuss things they feel important and seminal—it's [that integrity] missing here at present and there is no excuse for it to be missing....
> And 'til [critics] are prepared to make the drama desk a real challenge and a real lifetime's work, I don't think one can listen too carefully to what one reads in the papers.[96]

Both of the above comments were made in 1981, and Nicky obviously felt a great deal of security in making this kind of public statement on CBC. Most actors are very careful not to take on the critics. Nevertheless, an overwhelming number of Nicky's reviews contained positive and generous commentary from reviewers, both local and national.

When Nicky's resumè is assessed—over 250 television productions, seventy-seven roles at the Stratford Festival, his performances in Chicago and at universities, and seven films—the final tally is truly remarkable. Much of this was due to his work ethic. He once said he admired young actors who went to Toronto and waited for parts, but his own policy was to take whatever was offered. He was employed all the time, partly because work begets work—the more you perform (or teach), the more people see you and want you to perform for them.

In addition, Nicky was a great entrepreneur and motivator. If the roles he was getting onstage were not always quite as glamorous as Hamlet, he was still out there with one of his one-man shows, making sure he was in the public eye. Many of these began as small endeavors and after he worked on them and polished them, they got invited into a season of the Festival repertory. He also encouraged novice playwrights and would work with them to put a new piece together, offering advice and performing sections of the project. He had a gift for selling himself and for selling theater.

Nicky also developed and matured tremendously as an actor. Eventually he worked his way through the juvenile roles and directors began assigning him more and more challenging roles like Iago and the Fool in *Lear*, roles that might have been considered against type and out of his line of acting had he not done so well with them. Finally, he moved into deep, rich characters like Leonard in *Virginia* and Magnus Eisengrim in *World of Wonders* where he had a responsibility in creating the role.

In Nicky's private papers were dozens of letters from admirers which began, "I've never written a fan letter before, but…" Then the writer would go on to detail his or her number of years attending the Festival and number of times seeing Nicky's work and then expressing how this role (the roles varied a great deal from letter to letter) was clearly definitive.

His friend and colleague Martha Henry made this uncommonly perceptive summation after he died:

Somewhere inside him, he settled the dichotomy of what he started out as, the phenomenally gorgeous, *iridescent* leading man, who then became the elder statesman of the theatre. He could have been a major international star. But he chose instead a much more private surrounding at Stratford. He believed in the idea of a theatre company. His nature pointed in that direction: He wanted to contribute to something, rather than devote all his time and energy in the race to be a star... . I think there was a part of Nicky that wanted to hide away from the world. He didn't go to the bars or to the pubs after rehearsals. He could have gone anywhere he chose. Well, he went where he chose. That was to Stratford.[97]

He said repeatedly, "Theatre is really where my heart lies." This was the art form he preferred, this was his fulfillment:

It does surprise me, it seems such an incredibly short space of time. God, I've been lucky. I've played some enormous roles here. I've stretched tremendously. I've been given a chance to do things I never dreamed... . It's been a great gift.[98]

He made that statement in 1984. He would repeat it to his friends shortly before he died.

Early family photo of Nicholas, Robin, and Betty Pennell.
(Family photo, courtesy of Robin Pennell)

Nicky splashing on a summer day
(Family photo, courtesy of Robin Pennell)

Nicky dressing up
(Family photo, courtesy of Robin Pennell)

Nicholas Pennell as Jaques in *As You Like It*, 1983.
Photograph by David Street.
Photos courtesy of the Stratford Festival of Canada Archives.

Nicholas Pennell as Hamlet in *Hamlet*, 1976.
Photograph by Robert C. Ragsdale.
Photos courtesy of the Stratford Festival of Canada Archives.

Nicholas Pennell as King John in *King John*, 1993.
Photograph by Cylla von Tiedemann.
Photos courtesy of the Stratford Festival of Canada Archives.

Nicholas Pennell as David Frank in *A Variable Passion*, 1982.
Photograph by Robert C. Ragsdale.
Photos courtesy of the Stratford Festival of Canada Archives.

Nicholas Pennell as Leonard in *Virginia*, 1980.
Photograph by Robert C. Ragsdale.
Photos courtesy of the Stratford Festival of Canada Archives.

Nicholas signing autographs.
Photographer unknown.
Photos courtesy of the Stratford Festival of Canada Archives.

VII.
The Play's The Thing

ONE OF THE MOST INTERESTING PRODUCTION EXPERIMENTS in Nicky's career was conducted by Robin Phillips in the 1976 season when he cast both Monette and Pennell acting Hamlet in alternating performances. Phillips' rationale was that he had two potential Hamlets in his company, and he felt both should have a chance at the role since the play did not rotate into the repertory season that often. The remainder of the cast would be virtually the same for both productions except for the role of Gertrude: Nicky's Gertrude was played by Pat Galloway and Monette's by Pat Bentley-Fisher.

John Pennoyer's design concept had the players in Elizabethan (with traces of Carolinian) costumes executed in blacks and greys. The set built of rough, dark boards, designed by Daphne Dare, was intended to resemble the Festival Theatre's thrust stage, even though the company's performances would be given at the Avon, a proscenium arch theater.[99] The production was scheduled to tour on a Canada Council grant in Kingston, Montreal, and Ottawa for just over a month prior to its opening in Stratford.

Both actors approached the project with a genial sense of humor and a great deal of maturity, belying the pressure put on their mutual talents. Monette regaled reporters with his story of performing Hamlet at age 19 in Montreal, a traumatic

116

event at the time. The morning after his debut, he looked at the reviews. To his horror, one began, "If your name is Richard Monette, do not read any further," after which the critic proceeded to razor Monette's youthful and exuberant performance, his first time playing a leading role. Monette noted, "When I look back on it all now, it emerges as a sort of horror picture... like I Was a Teenaged Hamlet."[100] Monette was frank and forthcoming about his paranoia. When he accidently stumbled onto Pennell in full-dress Hamlet costume after a photo session, he thought:

> "What is this?" is what was going through my mind. God, it was as if I had opened my bedroom door and found my lover with someone else. I couldn't have been more upset. This was my role, the one I'd been living and struggling with. And then Robin said we should probably see each other's Hamlets, and, no thank you very much I didn't want to do that at all.[101]

Nicky was generous and open about what he had seen once both actors attended, very late in the process, one another's rehearsals. He recounted the differences as he saw them at that juncture:

> Richard is a Hamlet I could never be, and I suppose I'm one he could never be.
> I tend to be more romantic; I tend to hold back on the immediacy of my reactions, my shock at events....
> Richard has a sense of immediacy; he reaches very strong emotional conclusions in almost a film-actor's style. It's an extraordinarily, and quite rightly, modern Hamlet, a very naturalistic Hamlet.[102]

Oddly enough, Nicky did not see in himself some of the key qualities that Phillips knew would provide the tremendous difference between the two men's interpretations. His training among other iconoclasts at RADA in the late 1950s had made him think he was of that plebeian ilk. After David Warner's 1964 callow-youth performance of a Hamlet clearly in his 20s and clearly a student, the classical renditions of the role—most notably exemplified in John Gielgud with the beautiful profile and the sonorous intonations—had begun to be challenged. Pennell, with his English backgrounds and his blond good looks (now known to audiences which had just watched *The Forsyte Saga* in the early 1970s) came closest to this "romantic" or "poetic" stereotype. Nicky hadn't noticed: "Hamlet belonged to another school altogether and I felt I had none of the qualities to play him Gielgud said were necessary: the voice, the intelligence, the wit. It just never occurred to me the part would ever be offered to me."[103]

There were tangible differences between the two actors. Pennell was tall and English and slim; Monette was shorter and stockier and dark-haired, of Italian heritage. Monette was witty and social and reacted to events immediately; Nicky was more of a loner and more considered in his opinions. Monette was aged 31 and just beginning to get leading roles, Nicky was 37 and slightly more experienced in his acting career.

Yet, both were very solid friends and this general amiability aided them in surviving the natural crisis of being cast in the same role, Nicky as a kind of classical English prototype and Monette as what he called "a Renaissance man, moral, righteous and good. . . a Ralph Nader type."[104] The two were enormously loyal in complimenting and supporting one another in newspaper stories where the press had a field day drawing comparisons.

Both men also reiterated what is by now a commonplace—
that since Hamlet is onstage for most of the play (excluding
those few moments when Ophelia goes mad), the persona is a
"personality role," forged out of the genetic mix that creates
the disposition and temperament of the actor. Although every
role is that to a certain extent, Hamlet is twice so.
Consequently, if there are personality differences, as these
two men exhibited, the outcome will quite naturally be two
different interpretations. Monette stated:

> T.S. Eliot called Hamlet the Mona Lisa of dramatic
> literature. I like that. Hamlet is like an enormous
> puzzle with a piece missing and I guess every
> actor who ever plays him tries to supply that
> missing piece.
>
> You apply Hamlet's problems to the problems
> in your own life. One has to take a very personal
> approach in one's interpretation. It's also necessary
> to have tremendous physical stamina just to get
> through it. There have been days when I feel I'm
> in training for the Olympics. I don't think people
> realize the effort it takes. In actual fact, getting
> through the role requires the same amount of
> energy expended by a man digging a ditch for
> eight solid hours. And at the end, when you're
> almost totally exhausted, you've got the duel
> scene. It's the longest part ever written for an actor
> with, by actual count, 1,400 lines to be
> memorized.[105]

Nicky's explanation was characterized by Nicky's uniqueness:

> Primarily, I feel him to be a man of action who is
> suddenly shocked by his emotions into a state of
> inaction, caught like a fly on flypaper.

119

The difficulty for me has been to learn to play out all that emotion. I've always felt it was rather vulgar to get on a stage and show powerful emotions so nakedly. But Robin has taught me how to release this inhibition and for the first time in my life I think I've learned from him how to be truthful in expressing deep emotion without being vulgar.

.... He waited and watched until we... each came up with something that was uniquely our own... something that came closest to expressing our very own different personalities and when that happened that's what he developed as our interpretation.

The best way to explain it perhaps is to say he acted like an orchestral conductor directing a piano concerto. A case of two performances of the same concerto with two different soloists.[106]

In the actual performances, Nicky went for the Oedipal approach popularized by Olivier's 1948 film, a kind of love-hate longing for Gertrude, on whom he planted a lingering kiss during the closet scene. Monette's volatility and outwardness of emotional expression was noted and commented on by Nicky himself, who declared his admiration for that and added that Phillips was helping him manifest his own feelings onstage. Monette's Hamlet used a real prop notebook in one soliloquy ("My tables, meet it is I set it down") and Nicky indicated that he was recording in his mind and not actually writing. One newspaper made a huge brouhaha about the use of the skull Hamlet holds in the gravedigger scene. This reprinted conversation typified the humours of the two men:

". . . We have two skulls," [Monette] said in a joint interview.

"Why?"

"We each wanted one for the mantlepiece at the end of the season," Monette said. "I wouldn't want to play with Nicky's skull—yecht. I've got my name carved on mine. Nicky's has the loose top on it."

"We've got to get real ones," Pennell said. "If anyone has any extra skulls hanging about, we need two real skulls. Then we'd know from the molars which was which."

"I don't know," Monette mused. "I think it might upset me. We might get [the skull] of an actor and he might be putting lines in our mouths."[107]

Newspaper reactions for the length of the run were a case study in understanding the job of the theater reviewer who, after all, sees a single production of each show during the season: That night could be fairly typical of the performances or completely atypical of anything that had ever happened or ever would happen again. Both actors' performances were described, at different times, as "romantic" and both were labeled as "straightforward," a word which doesn't convey much at all. One reviewer ruminated:

But before we can take a real interest in his [Hamlet's] hemmings and hawings, we must first be convinced he really has it in him to do the deed—if he ever does decide on it. We must believe he has the potential to be king if he does dislodge the usurper. Otherwise, all his backing and filling is nothing but hot air.[108]

This same critic also observed that "Monette frequently seems to see farther into the role than Pennell, but Pennell is ultimately the more satisfying because he manages to let us see farther into it."[109] Whatever that means. Hemmings and hawings, backing and fillings, perhaps.

Sophisticated theatergoers, it has been noted, often have their own image of Hamlet; clearly, theater critics do as well. In fact, reviewers felt even more obligated to announce which actors did the best job (with the exception of one whose budget allowed him to see only 4 of the season's shows, so he chose only one of the Hamlets). During the tour, John Fraser announced that the production had promise but was not yet ready; he optimistically added that both actors were clearly not finished thinking about the role.[110] Gina Mallet, having seen the productions one or two days earlier than Fraser, gave her rendition of each performance:

> Monette is witty and romantic. Sometimes he even acts as if he were playing Mercutio, the dashing cavalier of Romeo and Juliet. He snaps with sarcastic relish; ill-concealed impatience fuels him. This Hamlet, one feels, would have not trouble fitting deed to action. He would have polished off Claudius and jumped into bed with Gertrude and be damned to everyone else. It makes for a lively evening, but ultimately a rather superficial one. Hamlet changes continuously, each soliloquy a revelation of altered vision, and the actor must let the man visibly ripen.
>
> Pennell is a naturally more introspective actor, and he speaks the blank verse much better. Monette tends to punch out the lines in two-word bites. But there is a shyness in Pennell; he never seems convincing as a man rocked to the core of his being. This is a nice boy who's gone astray,

taken drugs perhaps, and lost those English schoolboy manners that got him through so many scrapes before. However, as Hamlet becomes increasingly detached, Pennell gains in authority. He has a gentle speculative quality that makes a catharsis of the final bloodbath.[111]

At the end of a review which shows Mallet's bias to her own inner ideal, she heartily proclaims (as does the headline) that both men were worthy contenders for the role. Since these are reviews of early performances (and not on home turf), one would expect them to alter as each production grew. By the end of the run, critics were still choosing one actor over another, sometimes declaring Nicky the winner, sometimes Monette, handing the Prince's crown back and forth equally. A handful of reviewers declared that both were equally good or that both had strong points and weak points. Of course, Phillips and the actors (in what turned out to be quite exciting press coverage, almost overshadowing the fact that Maggie Smith was playing Cleopatra in the same season) encouraged everyone to see both productions.

The supporting cast did not fare as well as the Hamlets. One could not ever know exactly how they were directed by Phillips. Marti Maraden, as Ophelia, had given an interview early on, saying that both men were such different actors and such different characterizations that it made her job simple: "I simply react."[112] Other reviewers chose between Gertrudes, for the most part loved Polonius, and disparaged Claudius. For me, this last point was essential. The characterization of the usurping king was bland and mild and almost without villainy on the videotape that I watched (which was, admittedly, so badly lit as to amount to a radio version) that I wondered what tenacious magic it took for both Hamlets to get the play off the ground each night. Hamlet is very difficult to perform if the actor hasn't the required antagonism from the "mighty opposite" that Claudius should provide in the production.[113]

Perhaps to emphasize that these two men were suggesting two different acting styles during a transitional period in the history of performance, they were also cast as Caliban (Monette) and Ariel (Pennell) in the concurrent production of *The Tempest* with William Hutt as Prospero. As the ironies continued to double and froth upon themselves, fair winds blew from the *The Stratford Beacon Herald*: "Ticket sales at the Stratford Festival hit the two-million-dollar mark two months to the day earlier than last year." This was announced on 26 May 1976, 12 days before the opening of the show.

A second fascinating production experiment was Robin Phillips' direction of Edna O'Brien's script *Virginia*, a collage narrative of Virginia Woolf's personal life that was not crafted in the usual realistic playwriting mode. Almost a stream-of-consciousness theater piece, it focused on the artist's relationships with her husband Leonard Woolf, former colonial administrator in Ceylon, statesman, and co-founder of the Hogarth Press; on her budding love affair with Vita Sackville-West; and continued to her filling the baggy pockets of her cardigan with heavy stones and drowning herself in the Ouse. Virginia was played by Maggie Smith, Leonard by Nicky, and Vita Sackville-West by Patricia Conolly. The production opened at the Stratford Festival on 10 June 1980 and later transferred to the Haymarket in London [England] for a run of four months in 1981.

The reviews in Stratford were glowing but those in London were somewhat mixed, with most of the negative ones complaining about the play itself, almost as if critics could not accustom themselves to the structure of it. What the production decidedly achieved was a complete resuscitation of the career of Maggie Smith who, prior to this performance, trapped in the mold of comic actress. *Virginia* sealed her a place within the realm of the acting aristocracy, able to conquer a wide range of roles both classical and modern. At the opening night in Stratford alone, 82 critics were seated in the audience, from the U.S., Canada, and London.

Of the London critics, John Trewin lamented the fact that he did not know more about the Bloomsbury circle but declared this performance proved that he had undervalued Smith in the past. He praised her work, "fortified by Nicholas Pennell's watchful husband Leonard."[114] Michael Coveney, clearly enraptured by the performance and the play, exuded, "Above all, you get the sense of a spirit, wild in its small way, bursting to be left alone... and leaving a heart-broken and puzzled Leonard to get on with his life and work."[115] Michael Billington added, "Nicholas Pennell also deserves mention for his fine performance of Leonard, filled with bewildered love."[116] John Barber seconded this opinion, "A self-effacing Nicholas Pennell creates in Woolf a man who relished the gaiety and wit of his companion..." and closed his review with a comment about Smith: "Her return is most welcome."[117]

Although Francis King complained about the play, he declared that Maggie Smith saved it as "she glows and glimmers like some outsize opal, its mysterious fires perpetually changing colour." The reviewer added, "Though I never saw Leonard Woolf in a suit so well-cut or pressed, with half-closed eyes, I could almost believe in Nicholas Pennell's performance, that he had returned, with his characteristic tremors, from the dead."[118]

A first-night present for Nicky from Richard Monette was characteristically sly—a tote bag stenciled "VW," which contained a carefully folded but somewhat damp cardigan, the pockets full of large rocks.

More Memoirs:

Nicky left many examples of his thoughts about individual roles and character relationships, comments on specific productions, amusing incidents, and general opinions about performance and theater. Some of this commentary follows, supplemented by remarks from friends and colleagues. All are anecdotes and reflections which show another side of the actor.

ON PLAYING *HAMLET*, 1976

... In the early January of 1975, we were in the second week of rehearsals for *Comedy of Errors* and *Two Gentlemen of Verona*... we broke for coffee one morning. Robin and I were in the Avon lounge and we went through to look down at the stage. He said, 'Nick, I want you to play *Hamlet* next year.' Well, I nearly fell off the steps because we hadn't opened these two plays yet!

To some extent not prepared, I was the right age to play it [age 37]. I identified passionately with the text because there is a Hamlet in every one of us, a particular Hamlet.... .

Richard's Hamlet [Monette] could not have been more radically different... Italian, Quebecois, a sensibility so utterly different from little old middle-class English me.... Robin made us watch each other rehearse although we very much resisted it. I think it was hard, but that was a good thing. I know watching Richard that I felt certain choices were most extraordinary although I couldn't have made them. It made me more secure....I did not sit there saying 'I wonder if he does that better than I do.'

....

.... It's fourteen years ago, and considering that I'd only played three or four Shakespeare roles at that point, and that

Robin gave me the luxury of the full text... (Richard did cut his), the text has stayed with me as a kind of beacon so I return to it again and again.[119]

During the duel at the end of *Hamlet*... the danger is of course if you happen to be doing a fight with someone who is acting too much... because you have to just for a moment be terribly technical in what you are doing.... The temptation is, in fact, to nail Laertes—you really want to, but clearly, you can't. Be rather expensive casting if you nailed one every performance.

....

That role [Hamlet] for every actor is a kind of Mt. Everest. I would say mine got up to about the tree line.[120]

From Richard Monette: We had a preview and it was a packed house. When I got to the end of "To be or not to be" I heard a very loud voice in the audience saying, "Richard Monette, you are a bullshit actor." Of course, you are in such a psychological state when you're playing Hamlet because at that moment the character is contemplating suicide—and I thought, "I am losing my mind!" Of course, when something like that happens, the adrenalin shoots through your body. I turned and looked at Marti Maraden who was coming onstage as Ophelia to do the nunnery scene, and she was white and shaking. I thought to myself—What do I do now— have them bring up the house lights and have him ejected? And then I thought—What if he's right! So I went through the nunnery scene very, very quickly and threw Marti Maraden around like a frisbee, got off, and got a huge ovation.

Well, in the audience that afternoon was Carole Shelley, a great friend of Nicky's, who happened to be visiting him at the farm. After I went home, I immediately got a call from Nicholas. He said, "Richard, this is the actor's nightmare. This is terrible. What did you do?" And I said, "Well, Nicholas, I just paused and said, 'If you think I'm a bullshit actor, wait until you see Nicholas Pennell play this part!"

(Actually, this is an old joke about someone shouting "You're drunk!" to the actor playing Richard III, and he responds, "If you think I'm drunk, you should see the Duke of Buckingham!")[121]

From Stephen Ouimette: When Nicky played Hamlet, Richard Monette gave him an edition of the *Variorum Hamlet* which had inscribed in the front of it: "Dear Nicholas—You will need all the help you can get." When I played the role in 1994, Nicky gave me this same book and he wrote in it, "Dear Stephen—You won't need any help."[122]

ON PERFORMING IN *VIRGINIA*, 1980, 1981

The interesting thing about [playing that role] was that it was such a huge stretch. We played Leonard and Virginia at their optimum age, because Maggie played Virginia at the point of her suicide and I played Leonard at that point, even slightly older. I was playing a Jew of that period, a man who was an extraordinary literary figure in his own right but in some ways had eclipsed himself to enable Virginia to write. It was very exciting and so really outside anything I'd done before.[123]

By London standards, we opened to most extraordinary notices. When everyone else was down to two-thirds business, we had queues around the block.

The nature of the play itself—the major criticism leveled at it—was that it is not dramatically cohesive. This [criticism] is partially true—it is a pastiche, a vehicle, will not stand as a play, too much is avoided,… too near the subject matter… . Edna O'Brien [the playwright] used it as purely an examination of Virginia Woolf's life.

. . . Nonetheless its greatest value was to provide Maggie Smith with an extraordinary vehicle to let people see what had happened to her in six seasons in Stratford.... Amazing the number of people who came round and said,... this is a new actress, a different actress we haven't seen before.

I was having lunch with a producer with whom I was discussing the possibility of my doing something [in London], and he said with great respect and affection, "Look, I think it's absolutely splendid... your credential and the list of things you've done over there, but don't you think it's time now that you came back where the real theater is?" At that point I wanted to say, "I think your perception is not only blinkered to the point of blindness, but crazy."

. . . I think that probably one of the most satisfying [roles] for me, funnily enough, was Leonard Woolf because I loved playing it...because my job was to get inside the skin of someone who lived in my own time frame, who died when I was already a man, and who I felt I understood and I felt I kind of knew and recognized. And it was completely from the dark because [while rehearsing] I talked to no one and met no one who had seen him or knew him. So that anything I did was supposition from his work and from the relationship between the two of them and I somehow felt that I'd achieved some part of that, and when we were playing it in London, this is after playing almost more than a year of it [in Canada], I had a letter which I will treasure until my dying days.... That was the only time that external praise really mattered to me for longer than a fleeting moment.[124]

February 23, 1981

Dear Mr. Pennell,

I would like to congratulate you most warmly on your portrayal of Leonard. I think you have managed to convey exactly his special charm—stolid, compassionate, common-sensical, chunky, trembling and amused—and it seemed to me that your dialogues with Maggie Smith formed the most true and tender part of the play, in contrast to her faintly hysterical monologues and her over-dramatic scenes with Patricia Conolly, which lacked exactly this quality of tenderness that I remember.

For I must explain that I am Vita's son, and I very often saw all three characters together in life.

If I were to try to describe the Leonard-Virginia relationship, I would be very close to your imaginative reconstruction of it.

I have also edited Virginia's letters, and feel I know her and Leonard now far better than I did then. Your grasp of so sensitive a man is perfect, and as there are few people now living who saw them together in London and at Rodmell, I wanted to tell you so.

Yours sincerely,
Nigel Nicholson[125]

I bought a book in Charing Cross Road, it was years ago when I was doing *Virginia* in London in 1981. I bought a copy of *Orlando*, an early edition with the photographs of Vita, for about £4 or £5, not very expensive, and one of those little cards fell out... I looked through and a gray envelope with a New York postmark also fell out. It held one sheet of paper, dated 1942 with a West 57th St. address, typed on one of those old Underwoods. It said, "Dear Miss Lust: I am writing to inform you that my husband has been unwell so he has been unable to read *Orlando* by Virginia Wolfe as he is working on another

130

project. Yours sincerely, Carlotta O'Neill." It was a letter written just when O'Neill was writing the last draft of *Long Day's Journey Into Night*. To have found a copy of *Orlando*, which had obviously slipped through all those nets. There would come a time when it would be the perfect opening night gift, and of course there it was, after all my years of working with Martha Henry when she opened in this play in 1994. I must say she was thrilled.[126]

ON PLAYING IAGO, 1979

... A very serious side of me wanted to explore... the richer aspect of humanity. My first big chance was when Robin wanted me to play Iago, because nobody ever sees me as that kind of actor.... I began to realize that every preconception that one had about villains was inaccurate, that villains are heros and heroic themselves... Iago, Richard III, Stephano... all those roles became a real crusade for me to say to an audience—These are not villains. These people are you as much as the so-called heroes. Holding the mirror up to nature is two-sided.[127]

From the very beginning of playing Iago... I read the text a lot, just kept reading it. I kept thinking that no one in Shakespeare ever lies to the audience. Do they? He may lie to other characters but he always tells the audience the truth— either in soliloquy or in scene. Shakespeare's never dishonest—the text is the subtext in Shakespeare, if you see what I mean.... One has to have subtext because that is where a lot of the construction of the part sits.... So, when Iago... says three times that Othello has had an affair with Emilia, it isn't enough to say that he's condoning himself, that is a kind of modern gloss. From that point, I thought—Does Iago believe it, does he think that is the case? If so, then what follows? If he has more than a suspicion but less than a certainty that Othello has slept with her, then I begin to understand why he's doing what he's doing—the Cassio business, for example. I kind of understand his under-reasons.

Then there is textually the ironic wit and the charm and the astonishing vibrancy of mind that he has. He's not dull, he's funny—the mind goes like a rocket, you are fascinated by him. Again and again, I came up against the truthful, charming, attractive qualities—the areas in which he was hurt and operated out of a position of being tragically flawed. It's not just Othello who is tragic.

The more one perceived the audience drawn into the play, the further the audience went with you, the further they identified and said, "Now I understand him." When you go to the scene [where Othello has the fit], their revulsion grew out of their identification with Iago. And if they don't identify with Iago really, really strongly—and therefore with me as I am playing him—then the mainspring of the play is lost.[128]

It's terribly blinkered to say that anybody could write a protagonist that is all bad. I mean, what's interesting about that!

The only thing I could do when I played Iago was to find the man's humanity. The other choice would have been to make some kind of statement about his rottenness, his evil....I had to care for Iago. If it's just a man being extremely evil, Othello looks a fool![129]

ON PLAYING ANGELO, 1985

. . . Angelo [in *Measure for Measure*] was the most recently challenging because it was the last thing I did and because I discovered that it is one of the shortest leading parts in the canon. I found it the most incredibly tiring thing to do because Angelo goes through no catharsis. He's trapped completely. Even Macbeth has some kind of catharsis even though he is utterly alone. Angelo never resolves anything. To play a 35-minute scene with seven lines, and to be in fact the pivotal character on which the whole action revolves and is set, is extraordinarily tiring... .

Really the whole reason behind doing *Measure for Measure* the way we did it, and in the time we did it, was because it addresses the major problem of our time... we have completely lost respect for the authoritarian figures in our lives. We no longer trust the church; we no longer trust the legal system; we no longer trust the politicians. We have been consistently lied to, cheated, been forced to gaze on people whose double standards [have] become almost untenable... . You are dealing with a play that is speaking straight over 400 hundred years to the present time:

...But man, proud man,
Dress'd in a little brief authority,
Most ignorant of what he's most assur'd
His glassy essence, like an angry ape,
Plays such fantastic tricks before high heaven
As makes the angels weep...
[*Measure for Measure*, II.iii.120]

For the seduction scene I had to find out my own core of violence, and that was a very unpleasant thing. . . that scene always tore me apart. I used to come off and shake for five minutes afterwards. Purely because one had to look squarely in the face of the fact that at the heart of all of us we have a very, very, dark, sexually-tortured part of us. We can't avoid that, no matter how well adjusted we are and God knows most actors are not well adjusted.[130]

When I did Angelo, I was completely struck by the awful fix that he is put into—and given the circumstances and given the man—he is a victim. Also that he is manipulated unmercifully by the Duke. The difference [between productions in the 1970s and productions in the 1980s] is that instead of the Duke being a *deus ex machina* who organizes everyone's lives for the good, he becomes the Duke of Dark Corners, morally duplicitous. Angelo is indeed the fallen angel, a good person trapped into doing evil. I found that an absolutely clear window into the play—that one didn't have to excuse his behavior, which was only too human and painful. The agony of his act and then the rebuke at the end of the play, where he does not want forgiveness but wants to be punished finally for what he's done—he's forgiven in a way that is the eternal punishment where he is forced into marriage which he does not in any way desire. It's a very ambiguous play.

From Nicholas Rudall: I remember deeply the precision with which [Nicky] played Angelo... a kind of witted grace that he had. There was always on this wonderful face the possibility, in spite of his being the least cruel person I know, a dark cruel side to the character—so that it was always fleshed-out, complex, and layered. It wasn't just about language.[131]

VIII.
Yonder Cloud

THERE APPEARED A MELANCHOLY STAGE in Nicky's life which gathered around events at the end of 1985 and the first part of 1986 and continued for two or three years following. Thereafter, although his zest and enthusiasm for work continued—he'd found a new source of inspiration in working in Chicago—he never quite returned to the golden smiling self that everyone knew.

An early blow was the illness of his dog Gimli. Gimli was a bizarre and unlikely creature, a chunky black bull terrier. The dog accompanied Nicky on his marathon three-hour tramps throughout the countryside. Gimli was also the model for a dog-on-wheels brought onstage by the character of Moonshine ("and this dog, my dog") in a production of *A Midsummer Night's Dream*, so that the dog's outline, at least, is preserved as a "role model" in a property warehouse in Stratford. Stephen Ouimette described Gimli as a rather eccentric animal that put its face into streams, took out rocks, and stacked them neatly at the side. The dog was enormously loyal to Nicky but would not let anyone near his car or his property. If you were invited for dinner, Gimli would lie on the couch, farting at will.[132]

Although his partnership with John Williamson had declined, Williamson eventually moved to the United States.

By the early 1980s, Williamson had found a different partner, one who would not tolerate Gimli, the dog that John and Nicky raised together. Nicky eventually had made the difficult trek to the eastern United States to reclaim and retrieve the pet.

Alas, like all beloved animals, we usually outlive them, and Gimli died somewhere near the end of 1985. The vet came to his house and gave Gimli the fatal injection as the dog lay in Nicky's arms. He told Monette that he wanted to feel the sensation of death, with the animal there and then just not there. Nicky knew it was time for the dog to die and accompanied it to the end, always the hardest act, the most selfless act. The death of a pet is an inconsolable grief because there is no guilt, no dialogue, only pure sensation; Gimli's death was inevitably bound to the relationship with John Williamson.

Betty died in 1986, and although Nicky had an unusual relationship with his mother—one that he and Pat Galloway used to laugh about, the silent battles fought over Christmas dinner as Mum knocked back another drink—he nevertheless loved Betty deeply and was close to her when he was growing up. She held a unique, if complicated, place in his life. He reacted to her death with a mixture of guilt and confusion.

Yet another blow was losing the property he was living on in 1988, Kelly's Farm, because the landlord decided to give it to his son. Since this was a place where Nicky had been very contented, the incident counted as another stroke in a long list of difficult adjustments. In 1988, John Williamson died, not yet out of his forties. Nicky's mind must have been occupied with ineffable regrets, the narrative that might have been, the idyllic story of the farm at Tumbler's Bottom only partially realized and never fulfilled.

Monette claimed that the death of Nick's mother and then his dog inclined him to brooding thoughts. After Gimli's death, Nicky said that it was difficult to believe in an afterlife.

He had a couple of flirtations with Anglicanism, partly connected with his working on *Murder in the Cathedral*— Thomas Becket's crisis and Eliot arguing through these issues were just the kind of preoccupations that would have engaged his philosophical proclivity. Monette related that it was difficult for Nicky to perform in the production because he kept saying, "I don't believe this." Nearer his own death, when asked what kind of memorial services he would like to have, Nicky stated simply that he did not believe in a life after death and did not want church services.

The dark interval is reconstructed from information given by Nicky's close companions. In his personal papers at the Stratford Festival Archives, there were jagged and annoyed remarks, especially after 1985, in his professional mail because people tried to contact him, both by telephone and by mail, and had not been successful. Monette and Galloway reported that he would not return messages or answer the telephone, even when he was at home. He lost touch with both friends and colleagues. Director David Williams chided him in 1989:

> More to the point, Nicky, I can't with an easy conscience condone the plural inconvenience to which your incommunicado insistence subjects so many people, not least the stage-management, whose burdens I am seeking in as many ways as possible to alleviate. Beyond that, however, I believe that I and my colleagues in the management have the right to daily access of communication with all members of the company. I have therefore, asked Colleen that when she comes to negotiate your contract for next season some clause is inserted whereby this problem is solved.[133]

There is also an undated note from Robin Phillips which hints at some dissatisfaction within the company, quite possibly with some of the roles Nicky was being offered:

> Dear Nicholas,
> You sounded hurt on the phone. Enjoy your two days [away] —You are too important to be treated like this—important to Stratford and important to the world theater scene. Important.
> Much love,
> Robin[134]

John Broome commented about the malaise and indicated that it continued beyond 1989:

> There were moments in certain warm-ups where he was depressed or something. He would create a very dark atmosphere around him, and we'd be thinking where's that joyful Nicky? It wouldn't last, even though it would be very strongly there. I never queried, or asked, "What's the problem with you?" You didn't do that. You just sort of said this is the state he's in at the moment and he'll get over it. The next time you saw him he'd be laughing and joking again and enjoying every minute of what he was doing.[135]

Both Richard Monette and Stephen Ouimette talked about Nicky distancing himself from them. Even after Monette bought him an answering machine, Nicky would not return calls. Monette said, "I was not enraged, you understand, I was just angry with him. Because I missed him, you know, just to phone and things." Ouimette had also returned to Stratford and was unable to reach through the veil of silence. He left a number of telephone messages but Nicky answered none of them.

As he got older, Nicky believed that he got worse rather than better about communicating and sometimes felt less equipped to cope with life's problems. In discussing "the wound" in an interview in 1995, he generalized from his work outward to his life:

> Well, I find that [staying open] is the grave problem in one's life as one gets older. I've just come out at the end of a ten-year relationship and it has turned me very reclusive. For instance, I don't think I went out twice this year for a drink after the show. I find that I'm very turned in at present. And find that the only way I can deal with this particular hurt is not to expose it in any other place except in the work, if that makes sense....[136]

He went on to discuss what one begins to feel as one ages, diminishing potency in maturity, and his internalizing in an unhealthy way, but he also felt "it's the only way I can go." He went to his usual places for comfort, and interestingly enough, those places were Shakespeare's:

> .... We talked earlier of the ongoing and constant renewal of nature. Nature and art. The absolute renewing and refreshing quality of being in the midst of natural surroundings, of living in the country, of seeing seasons move, of wildlife, and all those things actually are extraordinary. Now I realize why they were so important because now is the time when I'm really using them to build strength.[137]

One of the things that Nicky spoke about in my interview with him in 1994 was the astonishing objective of memorizing T.S. Eliot's *The Four Quartets*. What was surprising was the feat of doing that project, the sheer mental kilowatts it took to put a piece of literature that large, that labyrinthine, even that repetitious—into his memory bank. Viewing the arc of his life in retrospect, he'd been working on the project for a number of years, having performed some of it with Marti Maraden. Also, the piece pervaded the research material about him. He would work his way up to one of life's mysteries in a particular interview and suddenly the subject was only explicable via Eliot, only a quote from *Four Quartets* would express the dilemma appropriately. On November 11, 1994, he achieved the poem. He offered a one-hour recital in Stratford Festival's Rehearsal Hall #3 and invited everyone in the company to attend.

At one point, Pat Galloway attempted to penetrate Nicky's isolation:

> We'd always spent Thanksgiving together, always. He was troubled, he really went into hiding, and he wouldn't even answer the telephone, not even for his closest friends. So I ended up writing a letter. I said, "Look—I love you and this is why I'm saying this. For goodness sake, what's the matter? Why this silence? You mustn't do this to your friends." I made all this a particularly personal thing, saying I shouldn't have to write.
>
>   Well, all of a sudden he phoned up and said, "Can I come for Thanksgiving?"
>
> All this happened latterly, not just before he died. He was troubled and went into a reclusive state. I've got all sorts of ideas about what the root of it was. He went through a period of being so solitary. Rather worrying, you know?[138]

Eventually, Nicky emerged as happy and relaxed. In fact, Nicky had taken the Frischke's (Pat Galloway and her husband Bernhard Frischke) out to dinner before they returned to their house in Portugal in early December, 1994. There was some talk of his visiting them there. Also, he was really looking forward to doing *Sleuth* in Chicago, especially after his great success with *Not About Heroes*. Everyone thought he was in wonderful form.

The final play Nicky performed was at the Court Theater in Chicago, a two-person psychological thriller by Anthony Shaffer called *Sleuth*, in tandem with his friend David New. It opened January 17, 1995, and was set to run until February 12. The notices had been very good. New provided these details:

> His back had gotten sore, and he went to see a chiropractor. The set had stairs to a landing which were difficult to negotiate, so we adjusted the blocking to help. We were three weeks into the run, but the performances just drained him. He would sleep on a cot until right before the show, then he'd be back on the cot during intermission. He'd get winded pretty easily.[139]

Nicholas Rudall added to the story:

> The play was all about transformation, two people playing different roles, a modern detective thing. That was when he started to know he was ill. At first, he was at dinner at my house, and he said he had a pain in his back. He thought it was due to climbing up and down stairs. The pain got worse, and he finally said to me, "You know, I'm not sure I can keep on doing this. I think I've put my back out." So we arranged for him to see a physician.[140]

Roy Brown recorded the following sequence in his diary. Nicky was driven from Chicago to Stratford and arrived in the evening on Thursday, February 2, 1995. On the next day, he had a doctor's appointment and was put into the hospital to remove fluid from his lungs. He was released and went home to Whitney Farm (at Brunner, outside Stratford) but discovered that the pipes in the house were frozen, so he went to Roy's house. Thursday, February 7, was a long day of X-rays and tests, and more fluid was taken from the lungs; this was followed by extensive bloodwork, a bone scan, and CAT scan on Friday, when the doctor informed him he had lymphatic cancer and that he might live from two months to a year longer.

Richard Monette came out to the house on Saturday and Nicky gave him the news that he would not be able to perform in the 1995 season. Nicky returned to the hospital on Sunday to have more fluid removed from his lungs. On February 14, Pat Galloway called from the airport in England, en route to India, to inquire about Nicky's progress. That same day, the lawyer visited, and Nicky gave power of attorney to Roy Brown.

Nicky's internist put him into the hospital on February 15. He was, by now, very close to the end. David New commented:

> At one point, the doctors had discussed therapies with Nick. He told them that if these were going to get him back to work, fine, but if they were not, he wasn't interested in them.... It was swift, swift. And mercifully so. If Nicky couldn't be working, I don't think he wanted to be around.[141]

Earlier on, a notice placed by director Robert Beard had appeared in the Stratford papers stating that Nicky would appreciate well-wishers writing in care of the Festival rather than visiting the hospital. The flood of letters that arrived during his illness was startling, well over 200 in a short period of time.

These came from a great cross-section of supporters. There was a note on the back of two photographs (of Stratford's fall trees against stormy clouds) from a young person who had been terminated at the Festival. She said Nicky was the first actor who paid attention to her and that she had enjoyed their chance meetings at lunch. There was a note from Susan Lemenchick, Monette's secretary, who said that whenever she and Nicky met, he always asked about her children. There was a telegram from Judi Dench and another from Domini Blythe, both actors with whom he'd worked. Robin Phillips sent a note about Nicky's courage in letting everyone write, and expressing admiration for this gentle soul he'd loved. Stage designer Phillip Silver wrote about *Virginia*, that although he'd designed the set he wasn't really needed in the theater all those hours, but he took such pleasure in watching Nicky, Maggie Smith and Patricia Conolly explore the text that he wanted to remain. A note from Denis Johnston, publications editor at the Shaw Festival, said:

> "I can remember several times settling into my seat in that wonderful playhouse, seeing your name in the programme, and saying to myself, "Oh good! Nicholas Pennell is in this." I knew that whatever else would be going on, you would give me a full and intriguing and challenging characterization to follow throughout the play, and that I would leave the theater the richer thereby."[142]

Notes arrived from friends who knew Nicky casually:

> . . . You and Richard were at my apartment and you sat in my cane arm chair (dated 1800's)... you were in the midst of an animated story when the cane gave out and there you were with your rear hanging out the bottom. . . ."[143]

A large number of letters came from people who had followed Nicky's career over the years. Some had seen every single role he'd played and wanted to express their appreciation. The following message from a retired professor was especially eloquent:

> ...I have often thought of the theatrical profession as one of the healing arts with its capacity for providing such joy, for relieving one of the stresses and distresses of daily life on this fragile planet, and for its ability to lift the human spirit. I often wonder how many lives have been saved, how many despondences assuaged, by a transcendent performance. Over the years, you have provided many of these great moments, and we many who have had the privilege of experiencing such luster are eminently grateful to you.[144]

The following message arrived from Veronica Tennant, his co-star in the final television production he'd made for CBC, *Satie and Suzanne*:

> This letter, I have sent to you many times in my mind, and I send it to you now, with my heart.
> Dare I admit how scared I was before our first day of rehearsal? I found you, the seasoned man of the theater, radiating kindness, professionally generous, sensitive, meticulous, patient, inspiring! When I see the film... it's with a chuckle and a cringe! You shouldn't have let the director order me to pummel you harder.... You were so swift on your feet in the orchard scenes, that is why I resorted to hurling apples.
> The film is glowingly yours, and yours is the voice, woven through the threads of performance,

textured and fluid, revealing yet mysterious, I
can't imagine a more skilled or undivided inquest
of the enigma that was Satie and his music.[145]

A note from Desmond Heeley, designer at the Festival for
many years, and Nicky's great, great friend, recalled beautiful
moments:

. . .A dozen or so pictures popped into my head:
of taking *She Stoops to Conquer* photographs of you
and Pat among the daffodils at the farm.... the joy
and rewards of doing (so many it seems!) fittings
with you, what every designer dreams about!
Laughter and careful work—& from you, kindness
to all.[146]

Pat Galloway sent a long, long, letter filled with news and
events. She pleaded with Nicky not to be brave in the final
moments of his illness but to ask for relief from the pain. Then
she plunged in:

O dear, now for the really hard part... for some
reason or other it is most difficult to say strongly
felt things out loud.... I can see you cringing, but
what the heck. I want to be as accurate and careful
as possible about this.
Nicholas, I think I can remember every single
time John and I have ever seen you on stage from
your Ariel twenty some years ago, neither flesh
nor spirit, trapped in some nether limbo, through
Titus Andronicus chopping off your hand, for
heaven's sake (actually, I wish I could forget that
detail but there it is with stunning
conviction...indelible, in technicolor yet); to your
quiet, rueful speech to Roxanne [in *Cyrano de*

Bergerac] and all those myriad other roles great and small in between, Shakespeare, Molière, etc. etc. It's an awful, staggering lot. Yet I remember all (I'm pretty sure about this) to a degree, the great preponderance of them really very well, and some with astonishing absolute clarity. I can't say this about a single other actor. (I'm certain about that.) If my preoccupied noggin holds all this of your work, imagine how many others do, only more so. Millions. Anyway, I do believe that the ultimate test for any work of art is simply how well it is remembered, and by that measure alone you are a great artist indeed.[147]

What finer tribute could there be for an actor, coming from another enormously talented actor? There was just time for what Desmond Heeley called "gathering up," putting things together before he died, putting closure onto an exuberant, fulfilling life.

On the first day of rehearsals for the 1995 season, Nicky wrote this letter to his friends at the Festival:

My dearest company, stage management and crew,

I wanted to write something to you on the occasion of your first day, from one who, for the first time in 24 years, cannot be there.

Each year the miracle renews: we band of artists are released into the adventure again to renew the act of faith in the recreation of the spirit of imagination. For it is that unique gift that is ours (our joy and our sorrow too): to delve into the stuff of our lives, and dig up with absolute fidelity and accuracy our happiness, our ecstasy, our pain, our misery, our laughter, our ironies, our intimacies passionate and unidentifiable—hot or icy cold; all unguarded and uncensored, free and truthful—and, through the medium of the text, allow the audience to receive the transubstantiation of our truth into their truth, their reality.

To hold, as 'twere, a mirror up to nature.

For that is what we must do as artists: demonstrate the shared wholeness of the human condition to our audiences; in order that together we may arrive where we started from and know the place for the first time.

That demands from us, my hearts, courage, endurance, energy and commitment of an impossibly high order. But look around this rehearsal hall and take heart. A room more full of talent, generosity, wit, speed, laughter, thievery, meanness, ambition, chutzpah and Bill Hutt is impossible to imagine—unless Monette has stepped out for a cigarette!

My love, my passion, my bliss and my joy, and my pea-green envy are, and always will be, with every one of you.

Now, take Bill's hand, he's a stranger in Paradise! What are you waiting for? Fly, my darlings!

I love you,
Nick[148]

The letter contained it all—Shakespeare, Eliot, his faith in the art of creating onstage. Also Nicky's philosophy of performance and his felt reasons for the existence of theater. Writing from the point of the view of the company in addition to the point of view of the actor—he epitomized every ideal of his exhortation to them. From his passing of the torch in "Fly, my darlings!" right up to having the final joke on Hutt and Monette. What an exit.

Nicky died on the afternoon of February 22, 1995, less than three weeks after his return from Chicago.

The memorial service was held in the Festival Theatre the following Sunday. The company rose to the occasion. A large photo of Nicky with his dog Pook was placed on the stage along with a floral arrangement and a podium. Three solemn bells tolled, followed by the Festival's traditional trumpet fanfare backstage, which has been played at every performance on that stage from the time it opened. Monette gave "All the world's a stage" and a reading of Nicky's letter. After this, he began a list of some of the parts Nicky had performed. Five actors followed—William Hutt, Martha Henry, Marti Maraden, Colm Feore and Stephen Ouimette. Each added to the litany of roles begun by Monette and then read poetry and prose chosen from a gathering of Nicky's favorites, from *Winnie the Pooh* to Shakespeare. At the end, Monette read "Fear No More" from *Cymbeline*, and the bells tolled a final time.

The programme for the ceremony was entitled "A Celebration of the Life of Nicholas Pennell" and listed celebrants and musicians. On the cover was a photograph of Nicky at Brunner farm, with his arm around the galloping, joyous dog Pook, with a quotation from Eliot's *Four Quartets*. Later on, Nicky's ashes were interred in the family plot at the Stoke Gabriel cemetery in England.

After the funeral, Nicky's great friend Roy Brown, who took him to the end of his life and also adopted Pook, had the idea to return to England to plant two Canadian maple trees in memory of Nicky. There is one in the graveyard, and one at the home of his brother Robin Pennell.

All this recalled the words Nicky had spoken about one of his major stage triumphs, the title role in *King John*:

> More important, John is already starting to return to the land. All the history plays share an

absolute passion for the island, a physical longing for each part of it. For example, the samphire gathering in *Lear*—such a simple image but so accurate if you've eaten them—they're really rather good. There's something about little bits of stone and rock and leaf and earth that John constantly touches.

John begins with the image of fever and fire, "so hot a summer. . . my bowels crumble up." Then he sails into an extraordinary description of the northern part of England, straight up the Pennine chain. He speaks of dying and going out into those curlew-haunted wilds with only low-down trees and that coolness and freedom and sense of height and air you get: ". . . Let my kingdom's rivers take their course / Through my burned bosom; nor entreat the north / To make his bleak winds kiss my parched lips / And comfort me with cold. I do not ask you much: / I beg cold comfort."

That deliberate sinking back into the earth, the earth that gave form to begin with, the course of nature and the inevitable rotation of ashes to ashes and dust to dust....

Although reading the obituaries was a disturbing experience, primarily one which conveyed the size of the loss of Nicholas Pennell, it was overshadowed by the eulogy written by a Canadian giant, Robertson Davies. This grand old man of letters had worked with Nicky on the stage adaptation of the novel, *World of Wonders*. Davies' epitaph drew an accurate portrait:

. . . He was not a "star" actor, using that term to mean an actor who brings a "personality" to the stage and imposes it upon whatever part he assumes.... But there is another sort of actor, who conforms to the idea established by Stanislavsky, who gives richness to the whole play, whose devotion to that whole helps the other actors to give their best, and whose deep seriousness—not, of course, meaning solemnity—makes the play that combination of a fine text with fine interpretation which produces truly great theatre.... This is the true theatre artist, who combines a classical actor's training with high intellectual and psychological perception.

Nicholas' quality as a theatre artist of this kind enabled him to encompass an extraordinary variety of roles, from the charmingly ineffectual Gayev in *The Cherry Orchard* to the wise—and wily—Ulysses in *Troilus and Cressida*. In roles calling for imaginative scope, such as Oberon and Ariel, he moved like a chieftain on his native soil, and in Shakespearean plays of the mythic, Magian world his certainty of touch was unerring; anyone who saw the deeply moving scenes of recognition and reconciliation in *Pericles*, one in which Nicholas played the lead, has seen acting of a very rare order—the sort of acting which seems to lead us back through time until all time and all human experience become one, and we are taken into the world where the healing truth of myth is palpable....

His versatility was astonishing. He could even play those Voices of Common Sense in the plays of Molière, which can be such bores, in a way that persuaded us that reason was just as much fun as imagination. He could persuade us of the saintliness of Thomas Becket in *Murder in the Cathedral* and he could show us a man who thinks he has God in his pocket, like Malvolio. He could make Faulkland, in *She Stoops to Conquer* [sic], as interesting a study of amatory perplexity as young Marlow....

But to the lover of the theater at its highest reaches Nicholas Pennell was an unfailing delight, and the special warmth of applause that always greeted his appearance in the "general call" at the end of a performance was evidence of that, whether his role had been great or small. His loss is a loss indeed, for he was an artist of a very rare sort, and his death diminishes our hopes, though it leaves us rich memories.[149]

Davies' words capture the essence of the master craftsman, following Nicky's advancement from the competence and charisma of a player of juvenile roles to an utter command of technique and characterization in one of the most demanding performance spaces in the world. He acted and enlarged his own experience, he unfailingly watched other actors and learned from them, he was apprenticed to by younger talent. He passed the torch.

There were several gestures toward commemorating Nicky's work. Writers' Theater near Chicago changed its name to the Nicholas Pennell Theater on March 2, 1995. The press release announcing the name change carried this comment by Michael Halberstam:

In early 1995, we lost a great theatrical light with the untimely death of Nicholas Pennell. Known to many for his work at the Stratford Festival in Canada, his career was one of absolute devotion to art. Nicholas was a fierce advocate for the theatrical education of young actors and a firm believer in the power of the word, and in the spirit of his contribution we named our performance space for him.

This was especially appropriate because the enterprise specializes in producing performances based on the work of great writers, such as *Not About Heroes*, which had been produced by Artistic Director Michael Halberstam with Nicky playing Siegfreid Sassoon and David New playing Wilfred Owen.

A Variable Passion was performed in his honor. When Nicholas Rudall called Nicky in the hospital before he died, Rudall asked if there was anything he could do. At first, Nicky said no, that he was at peace. Then he said there was something—Rudall could direct David New in *A Variable Passion*: "And I promised him I would do that. And David played what Nicky wanted him to play" in March of 1995.

In the summer of 1997 when I was in Canada gathering material for this book, the Chicago Associates dedicated a director's box that they had funded, high above the Festival Theatre stage, to Nicky on August 9. The Chicago Associates were a group of angels (donors) who financed the apprenticeship of young Chicago actors for a season at the Festival. These apprentice performers were allowed to join the company and train as classical actors. Nicky, of course, strongly supported the program and often presented workshops for them as well as mentored them in Canada. Very few professional theaters have a director's box, a small room above the last rows of the audience in the Festival Theatre, fronted with windows, that can be used during performances for a director and guests—designers or fellow directors or actors or whatever—to view and discuss "in-progress" performances. Outside the box hung a remarkable pencil drawing of Nicky costumed in three different roles, rendered by Susan Benson, who frequently designed for the Festival. Also hanging there was his farewell letter to the Company and the eulogy written by Robertson Davies.

Finally, there was a copy of an elegy, not surprisingly, similar to the one written for Richard Burbage in the 1600s, the pre-eminent actor of the Lord Chamberlain's Men, Shakespeare's company in Elizabethan England, that was composed by Ric Wellwood, who had reviewed productions at Stratford for twenty-five years:

Where Pennell Played

I know this place, this space where great theatre has flourished.
It grows there still, and will for years, having nourished
The spirit of nearly half a century of people hungry for fun,
For laughter, challenge, a sense of occasion, but I, for one,
Call it the place where Pennell played.

He trod the boards for more than half its life, the trade his wife,
The language his mistress, the words honed sharp as a knife,
Cutting through confusion until the Bard was made simple and clear.
None could play this place without gifts, some made a career
In this place where Pennell played.

I've been at this place for twenty-eight seasons reviewing,
Enjoying the classic authors, discovering actors, renewing
A look at the greats, and those who never quite flowered.
From Ciceri to Hutt, Gascon, Hirsch and Hayes, he towered
In this place where Pennell played.
In all that time, through hundreds of trumpets and gongs,
Through all the companies, and productions and songs,
I blush to say that only three times the acting made me weep,
And it was Pennell who twice wrung those tears so deep
In this place where he played.

The first time in Pericles, in a poignant reunion he surprised
My introduction to this rarely done work, and then I surmised
It must have been something drunk at a lengthy intermission.
I couldn't be so touched by fathers, daughters and submission
In this place where Pennell played.

Much later, and more than once, he stood in the Avon, speaking
As a weary poet, battered, bruised, lost in history, seeking
The meaning in unspeakable carnage among damaged men.
There they go, the lump in the throat, the tears again,
In a place where Pennell played.

I could go on about the roles that stand among the great,
The Hamlet, the Goldsmith swain, the cogent Fool: mate
To one done by Hutt, for Hutt, the Puritan, the Knight,
The King with the hollow crown, the clown, the silly frown
In this place where Pennell played.

I've seen him with Bedford, with Smith, with Monette,
With Henry and Galloway and some I forget,
But it has been more than a career that I saw in this place:
It has been genius, humility, and matchless grace
In this place where Pennell played.

Yes, this has been the place where Pennell played,
And sure as the glow tape gleams on the boards
There are places where the wood glows warm with prints
Of the feet that carried a man of gifts, a Prince
Of the theater - Nicholas Pennell.
　　The allusion of the Prince, of course, was lost on no one—
among other things, a reference to the famous "Good night,
sweet prince," from the death scene in *Hamlet*.

IX.
He Was A Man For All That

NICKY HAD GENEROUS FRIENDS. In every interview I conducted, his companions recollected stories Nicky told and passed them on, so that in a delightful way, his sense of humor proliferated. Richard Monette relished the role of raconteur, getting involved in the tales and adding his own embellishments. One of the funniest was about a cruise Monette arranged. Cunard invited a number of players from the festival to travel along with the dozen or so passengers on a cruise through the Caribbean:

> We were doing some kind of show on board, *Rogues and Vagabonds*, I think, and at meals we would tell stories or just talk with people. Nicky and I were sharing a cabin and one night we were into our cups and we were shouting outrageously personal things to one another. Nicky never criticized me about my life except on this one night. We weren't fighting or anything, it was just high spirits. But it was very raw. The next morning we got up for breakfast with an enormous hangover and one of the passengers said, "My, you boys were certainly up late last night. I was in the cabin next to you and heard every word you said!"[150]

This story was corroborated by a letter sent to Nicky during his illness, which must have given him great pleasure. First the writer told him how long she'd followed his career, from *Forsyte Saga* to Canada, "with amazed delight that you had been lured to Stratford where we would be able to enjoy your talent live on the stage." She'd seen his Pericles, Orlando, Hamlet—"the year you alternated with Richard Monette, I think, with delightful rivalry,"—and also Ariel, Richard II, Iago, and his King John three times:

> I also have very happy memories of that dreadful boat trip we took in 1978, I think. The only good part was watching the performances you actors put on for the few people in the group and the joy of having the cabin next to you and Mr. Monette, and hearing you yell at him in great ire around midnight to tell him to wake up, you had not finished complaining about the appalling trip you had been inveigled into. Mr. Monette and I drank too many pina coladas, and flung ourselves on the floor when we had to stand in line for visas, hoping we would be rushed to the front and avoid shuffling along, and you turned to us and in a most scathing voice said, "Oh, get up. Just the behavior I would expect from you two!"

> . . . With very best wishes, Marian Stoddard[151]

Pennell and Monette had one of those long-lasting rare friendships where they played outrageous jokes on one another. Monette specialized in elaborate opening night cards that just missed complimenting Nicky on his performances. Another postcard punned on their having alternated the role of *Hamlet* and also on their appearance in *The Devils*, where Nicky played Father Urbain Gran and Monette played Sewerman:

Dearest Nicky:

We meet today not as Dane to Dane (as t'were)
but as priestly Dean to Drain! Have a great show.

Richard[152]

An interesting ambiguity about the *Hamlet* performances
that these two shared showed up in the interviews. Nicky
made a great point of saying to me that, although both men
resisted it, Robin made them watch each other rehearse.
Monette insisted in his interview with me, "We never
watched one another. The director wouldn't allow it." The
actual case was, as Chapter VII revealed, that the two watched
one another but only near the very end of rehearsals.

Of course, many of their stories were connected with their
work onstage and their long association with the Festival
Theatre. In a production of *Tempest* where Monette played
Sebastian, he had a line, "Now I will believe that there are
unicorns." John Hirsch was directing the show and kept
telling Monette, "I can't understand you." Richard tried the
line every conceivable way, putting in so much emotion that
he was almost weeping. Finally Nicky went up to Richard and
said, "What he means is he can't hear you. Just be louder."

Another time Richard was having trouble with a role and
sought out Nicky to find out what he could do. Nicholas gave
him this classic advice: "Be angry. It always works. No matter
what—be angry."

The two met when they shared a dressing room in 1973 for
a production of *Taming of the Shrew*. They were often guests at
one another's houses for Christmas because Nicky loved to
cook and would make a traditional English dinner complete
with plum pudding and all the trimmings. Nicky advised
Richard about cooking and gardening. He was a fountain of
knowledge on those subjects. When Nicky took Canadian

citizenship, Monette gave him a Charles Pachter cartoon of Queen Elizabeth II riding a moose.

Monette emphasized that the most important thing about Nicky was how much fun he was: "He was my closest friend for the longest time in my adulthood." In Nicky's last days in the hospital, it was part of the therapy to administer a wide range of drugs. He told Monette, "I'm sick enough as it is and now they're giving me estrogen. I certainly don't want to become pregnant."[153]

Nicholas' friendship with John Broome was based on mutual admiration. Broome had his own dance group and had experimented with using actors in dance productions. It had not escaped his notice that actors understood and interpreted stage movement much better than dancers, who seemed capable of working only in their own idiom. He contacted a number of drama schools about his ideas, and no one responded except John Fernald at RADA, whose movement coach had become ill. Broome filled in for him, and once Fernald had observed one class, Broome was hired on and stayed for nine years. So Broome and Pennell had known one another in their early careers in England and reconnected twenty years later in Canada. This mutual belief in training the body (and also the necessity for a stage choreographer for battle scenes and epic moments in theater) was a great commonality. There was a fruitful exchange and strong working relationship.

Broome once directed one of Nicky's scripts, *This Fair Child of Mine*, using young students in a drama school near Toronto. The boys played women's parts, Elizabethan-style. When Nicky went out to teach, he'd often ask John about an exercise they'd done in warm-ups. John took him through every step so that the exercise would be correctly employed and have the right effects in the classroom. They also did teacher-education workshops together where Nicky worked on text and voice and John did the body work. Once Nicky asked him for a page of exercises (to keep himself physically fit during the winter), and this regimen was preserved in Nicky's private papers.

The friendship carried over into their private lives. They both lived in the country, and Nicky visited with Pook on his long walks. He remembered that John was keen on ornithology and shared information about good bird-watching spots. John's wife and Nicky had a special kinship; she saved produce for him from the garden, "especially peas, he loved peas." Broome remarked that Nicky carried his script and his binoculars on long journeys through the woods.

Broome described a freaky car accident Nicky had. He'd been traveling home in his jeep, and as he was passing a large truck, a gust of wind caught him in its vortex and actually blew him off the road. Neither Pook nor he was injured beyond a broken thumb, but Nicky's first question was, "What's happened to my script?"

Broome recalled Nicky's favorite story about the woman in Suffolk who was trying to have the church organist fired. Her husband had been a butcher. At his funeral service, the organist elected to play that favorite old hymn "Sheep May Safely Graze."

Pat Galloway acted at the Festival from the early 1960s and by the time Nicky arrived in Canada in 1972, she was well-established in leading roles. They met at a party in London given by Glynis Johns:

> Penny (as I called him) and I were introduced because he was coming out here to play Marlow in *She Stoops* and I was Kate Hardcastle. I was sort of prickly and said, "I hope you're not coming to Canada to be all po-faced and British." (And here I am British as hell.) He probably thought, "Who's that cow — we'll see about that!" Anyhow we were soon fast buddies and we had a lot of really uproarious times.

> It was one of those friendships where we might
> not see one another for weeks—partly because we
> hadn't been cast in the same show so weren't
> working in the same building. Always on my
> birthday there would be a huge parcel of books,
> or a check left at the Garden Center for $100 worth
> of roses, that kind of thing. That's why when he
> alienated himself, we understood that he was in
> some sort of trouble and needed rescuing.
> He was a true friend.

There was one delightful Christmas when Pat Galloway and her husband Bernhard Frischke and Nicky rented a hotel near Devon, just over the border in Somerset. It was a small establishment so the party was just large enough to take over all the rooms. Nicky's relatives arrived, including Robin and Jenny Pennell and their children, a memorable holiday for this family grouping. Nicky left Pat two valued personal gifts when he died—a gold circlet which he always wore around his neck, and his signet ring. Another close friend, again connected through the work and through common intellectual interests, was voice coach Patsy Rodenburg. She had trained in voice in the 1970's in England yet she was always curious about the kind of craft (as she termed it) learned by actors in the generations that preceded her. Instead of considering the earlier elocutionary styles as outdated or old-fashioned, Rodenburg determined to explore and investigate the old school, partly because she worked with older actors who had completed their training at an earlier time. She apprenticed to the older teachers, people like Sheila Moriarity, to discover what had created this rigid and "held" school of performing, what its strengths were, its weaknesses. Since she respected that work, and subsequently tried to marry two schools of thinking about voice and technique, Nicky instinctively understood that she was knowledgeable about how he'd been trained:

That was one of the reasons Nicky took to me. I remember him just looking at me at the very first class—there was this enormous sense of relief, that somebody understood and had not abandoned a tradition that he thought was lost.

When I did classes for the young ones in the company, he would come along. I taught them things like how an iambic works and how you have to feel it and speak it. He was over the moon with those exercises. Of course, he did not need it himself. He just got on the wave and went.

Rodenburg also took to Nicky. She was a great admirer of the inner character of the man and described him, as did others, in her own way, showing several facets:

Nicky was a very handsome man, and yet he didn't really invest in that. It's very hard for people who are good-looking to relinquish that—you get rather sad actors and actresses holding onto the wrong things and not letting age enrich them. A great artist can't be vain—he has a humility that takes him beyond that. Nicky didn't mind what he looked like onstage—he didn't bother about those things.... If the character was elegant and gracious, then he was elegant and gracious, but he had no problem downgrading himself either. The play was the thing and the part was the thing.

Rodenburg spoke of personality traits:

He was a shy man... very discreet, always generous.... He was not withdrawn but he didn't necessarily socialize, didn't go to the bars nor drink too much, as some actors do. Which kept a sort of dignity about him. He was a good company member but he never let the boundaries cross between personal and professional. He was supportive of young actors, answered their questions and gave them tips all the time, at lunchtime or whenever, but he never misused that power.

I was very moved because he did, in a way, invite me into his personal life. The first year he took me around and introduced me—he was so kind to me personally. Such a gentleman, really.

He always had a sense of perspective, especially about the work. It has always amazed me that some of the most abusive people in the world work on these great plays of Shakespeare, which constantly teach us that we shouldn't misuse our power, that we should seek reconciliation. But Nicky did, you see—he took something from the work he did and carried it into his life. I would call it grace. He had grace.[154]

Nicholas Rudall had an affinity with Nicky because they shared parallel pasts. Rudall was Welsh and had arrived in the United States in the 1970s. He founded the Court Theater on the University of Chicago campus (after single-handedly raising $4 million to build it) and was Artistic Director there from 1981 to 1995. He had gone to the Stratford festival on an alumni bus tour. He met Nicky, and soon after they fostered the exchange with the young actors that became known as the Chicago Associates. Both Michael Halberstam, director at Writers' Theater of Chicago, and actor David New were once part of that group of apprentice actors.

Rudall suggested a reverse exchange, where Nicky went to Chicago to perform. He agreed and directed Rudall in *Macbeth* as his first project. This is one play, of course, from which many time-honored theater stories emerge. Soon the two friends were exchanging them and even adding to them—for example, the one about the actress who as Lady Macbeth made the letter scene look like a postcard—and the actor who garbled "The candles are all out\ There's husbandry in heaven" to "The husbands are all out \ There's candle-ry in heaven."

There was the famous afternoon when David New, as Donalbain, was supposed to run out on the balcony, shouting loudly—with his shirt off, since Donalbain was surprised at night—to announce the murder of his father, Duncan. Since this was a matinee for the schools, the young women in the audience showed loud appreciation whenever the handsome David appeared onstage. David informed Nicky backstage that the scene would be modestly done that day, with shirt intact. New ran out onto the balcony, Macbeth and Banquo down below looking up at him, with the shirt, oddly enough, slipping off one shoulder in what Rudall described as "a decolléte moment." David's line was "What's amiss?" Rudall was just able to choke out the response, "You are." The incident became part of their legend onstage.

Later Nicky played Henry Higgins to Rudall's Doolittle, a character Nicky quickly re-christened "DoTooMuch" as Rudall embroidered his role. The two friends enjoyed many gourmet meals together.

Nicky's privacy was something that all of his friends strove to protect. That respect is honored in this book as well. His dear friend Domini Blythe, in talking about him, emphasized his way of keeping to himself but yet giving to others when the right moment came. Nicky and Blythe both joined the company at about the same time, toured together, and socialized a great deal. About a month before his death—close to Nicky's learning about his illness, he contacted her and requested that she aid a young, fledgling director friend of his. She felt that was his way of saying farewell.

Nicky's close friend and faithful comrade was Roy Brown. Roy and Nicky had worked at the Festival roughly the same number of years. In the early 1970s Roy went to Sheffield in England along with Tanya Moisiewitsch to join a theater company being formed by Sir Tony Guthrie. Guthrie died unexpectedly. Roy returned to his work in Canada as head of properties at the Festival and subsequently spent many years working with both Moisiewitsch and Desmond Heeley.

To Roy fell the most difficult task of all, taking Nicky through the course of what both knew was a fatal illness. No one will know the extent of the work that Roy did nor will they fathom the depths of his pain. A diffident and retiring man, gentle and giving, he never talked about himself. He facilitated other people's lives and made few demands. He took care of Nicky's papers, he made sure that a small inheritance got to Nicky's family despite complicated legalities. He even negotiated the difficult transfer of the six rose trees on Nicky's back porch to their winter resting places in the yard. Finally, he took over the ownership of the rambunctious and warm-hearted Pook, a true labor of love.[155]

These friendships, or "mates" as they called themselves, produce a picture of a balanced life with support lines strongly interwoven into an extended family. All described Nicky and his life with great affection. He did the crosswords, he loved old films, he loved goofy television programs showing home videos, where people fell out of boats and got knocked over by pets. He read voraciously, at least four or five books a week. He set a goal to get through all of Dickens one winter and did it long before spring.

Nonetheless, the major part of Nicky's identity was his work, his notion of himself as an actor and, more than that, an actor in a large and successful company. In an interview in 1977, early in his career, he was asked to outline a typical working day, when rehearsals began in February and the season ended in November:

. . . Between the opening June 6 and the end, including matinees in high schools, I'm doing eight performances a week pretty consistently. There is the old belief that actors lie about all day. This comes chiefly from the fact that it takes a long time to wind down after a show. You may want to go out for dinner or go to a bar and have a scotch or whatever. Generally, I don't get to bed until half past one or two, so I don't get up until ten a.m. mostly. Then I have a house that needs to be taken care of in various ways....

During the rehearsal period, we have an hour's warm-up available every day.... Half an hour of voice work and half an hour of physical work.... I think it's essential. You can't go onto a stage, really, unprepared [so] it gives you a preparation period [so that] the body responds and the voice responds to the demands made upon it by the production.

[I'm] at present rehearsing a two-man show with Marti Maraden, which we will be taking around the States and various places. We're doing it under the Stratford banner and Robin's going to direct it. So we're rehearsing that most days from 1:30 to 4:30. I'm a member of the Casting Committee for next year, and I'm also a member of the Guthrie Award Committee....

I have two dogs that need to be exercised and entertained...I mean the days don't get empty even though one is not rehearsing.[156]

Work in the theater is labor-intensive, requires a great many social and collaborative skills, and is rarely overly remunerated. Nicky involved himself whole-heartedly and took on a great many tasks beyond acting. He recruited for the company, he represented them on radio and television, he often taught whatever group of young actors was in the Festival that year. His friends commented with admiration at the mantle of leadership that fell naturally onto his shoulders.

None of his extracurricular work ever got in the way of the quality of his performances, however. Broome emphasized:

> He was absolutely unflinching about his performances. He would never do anything that was slapdash or unconsidered or off the cuff....His acting was beautifully honed and polished and perfected, and he demanded that level of skill from all those around him. He'd got too much of an abundantly generous personality and sense of humor to allow anything to be niggly or whinging or behind backs.

Actor Janet Wright seconded this opinion about his professionalism:

> I felt a kinship with him completely. We did *King John*, it's the only time we ever acted together. I thought, well, this isn't much of a part—she dies after Act I. And she has very few lines. But I was so present in that performance because Nicky made me important. If you don't have an actor who endows you with importance, you could disappear completely. You don't get a lot of actors who create you. It was one of the best times I've had onstage.
>
> The thing about Nicky was that he was always learning. Some actors think they know it all and there is an atmosphere in the rehearsal room that is unpleasant because here comes so-and-so and they rule the roost because they already know how they're going to play their part. Nicky wasn't like that. He was a fellow actor, plus he had a great

regard and passion for the young people. He used to do a lot of work with them and that's part of the job.

But a lot of people don't do it.

Michael Halberstam once asked Nicky, "What is my job as director of Nick Pennell?" Nicky said "First, you must move the audience, then you must keep the pace going. Finally, you must stop me from being sentimental [onstage]."

Nicky had a tendency to be very business-like in rehearsal or at work, and then charming and amusing once the performance was over. Occasionally, people found this sense of compartmentalization alarming. It felt as if he were withholding something, as if he had a big box inside him that contained things not available to look at. As Halberstam said, he would tell you his past, but he wouldn't tell you his present: "That was still his private business and he wouldn't talk about that until it had been refined and articulated and polished up and made presentable to other people." It was still being constructed, being shaped into the narrative mode, readied for telling.

Marti Maraden saw a dichotomy that emerged over time, partly from the requisites of being on tour:

> [He had] absolute polar opposites of being one of the most sociable party animals I've ever known in my life—he'd take over after the performances. I'm a day person—Nicky was a night owl, marvelous at dealing with people, took that on very generously, took the burden of the social aspect of our partnership.
>
> In the same regard, when he seemed so extroverted, he was one of the most introverted, hard-to-know people, very private. We had dinner together, and I had to be careful because I wound up drinking more scotch than I was used to. Some

of our chats were very personal and I was honored to know that he was telling some things he wouldn't ordinarily tell....

But it took a long time to get to that point. I remember thinking: I know him but I don't know him. Maybe that's true of me as well... .

I think he had great happiness in his work, and I think that meant enough that he had a happy life altogether. On a personal level, there were great moments of pain and not a particularly happy life.

There was a sense of old-world gentility about Nicky, an unfailing, inherent politeness. For example, if you told him something in confidence, he maintained absolute discretion. You asked him not to tell, and he would nod his head and you knew he never would.

It is said that compassion is the highest form of human achievement. When Janet Wright lost her parents and her sister in a fire, Nicky was gentleness itself. He never probed or asked leading questions; he simply let her know that he was available. Many stories of this kind surfaced after he died. People remembered his comfort and his generosity, but none of this ever drew attention to itself. His example showed others how to live, juxtaposed the really true and exposed the fraudulent.

Nicky's periodic retreat from the world was logical. First of all, his working schedule was enormously full. He was in rehearsal or in workshops a good many hours of the day. If he was not involved in projects that drained his energies, he was engaged in getting there or going on to the next one. Teaching and performance are high-energy occupations, and hours onstage or in the classroom are considerably higher voltage than in other professions. Both actors and teachers need to re-charge and re-fuel, and Nicky was often involved in doing both these jobs on the same day.

He developed a philosophy that revealed his sense of service warring with his sense of artistry:

> "I've gotten into a pretty bad habit of now being ruthless about stuff that is either negative or that is of no value to me, which is not an easy thing to do because sometimes one should say, "This person needs at this point, for me to listen." But with the drawing on of day, and with the constant knowledge that time is running out, you think, I've got now to say, "Sorry, because I'm not the person, because there are other more important things I have to hear." It's very difficult, that.[157]

It is also very sane, that. As we age, we sieve through our actions and motions and cull out those that will not contribute to growth and forward movement, that would impede making a contribution. This is a natural stage. Yet the sifting is a struggle.

X.

Epilogue

IN THE SUMMER OF 1998, I visited Devonshire in the southwest of England, the location of Nicky's birth and youth. I took the train from London traveling toward the town of Exeter St. David. The sea was grey and stormy and choppy that afternoon, nonetheless covered with many boats, fearless sailors shouldering through the day. Sharp peaky rock clusters, slabs of craggy red stone, abutted the rails. The day grew more blustery and unsettled.

Jenny and Robin Pennell met me at the small station in Bovey Tracey and took me to their home. They showed me three satchels full of photographs of young Nicky, the various homesteads, more family and friends of Betty when she left her first husband and found a life with Gerry, finally settling down in Stoke Gabriel for twenty-two years of eventful life after Gerry's death. There were mostly black-and-white camera shots—Betty in a swimsuit sunbathing at the beach, the boys playing games nearby with the various dogs that were always part of the family, Betty's friends and drinking buddies Lupin and Rosie and Patty, Robin and Sebastian donning costumes for Nicky's entertainments, Robin playing with his pet monkey, photos from the local pageant at Compton Castle for the Queen's coronation year. Then more pictures of Nicky as he returned from drama school, cigarette in hand, the long, Carnaby Street skinny-pants of the late 1960s, extravagant poses.

There was memorabilia from a family that made claim to being part of the gentry, an assessment of the family silver Nicky had done in Toronto, stories and medals and newspaper features about the friends and relatives of Crockers and Folletts and Arundels and Pennells.

Jenny and Robin offered to drive me around the area to look at all the places Nicky was connected with— Goodrington, Marlden, Paignton. Down we flew between hedgerows fifteen feet high flanking the one-lane roadways, the bright green of them polished by the intermittent rain, the danger of this ride heightened by not knowing whether another car was looming around the curve. I saw the big house that Gerry and Betty lived in, could picture the boys putting flags out into the trees to welcome guests. I saw Windy Corner where Nicky sat all day entertaining the little old ladies as they waited for the bus. I saw the house Betty settled in at Stoke Gabriel, up a winding hillside in an assertive little English village much like a New England resort town.

We parked near the pub and made our way to the top of the hill, Robin commenting on the English custom of placing church and pub almost side by side. We spoke with the verger on the way up who sat on the porch of his little house, a squinty-eyed smiling man popping out short phrases, obviously a character model for Molière.

Then we stepped under a huge spreading yew tree, pinioned and trussed against its thousand years of age. There was a soft sighing that silenced our talk and quieted my dancing emotions: "We, content at the last / If our temporal reversion nourish / (Not too far from the yew-tree) / The life of significant soil." A magnificent surrounding view of the River Dart opened over the gravesite, the water steely grey and fringed with pines and those green divided rolling hills of

England. Nicky's gravestone contrasted with the others, dates like 1760, 1820, flashed on the left and right as we walked toward it. His was specially chosen by Robin and Jenny from a friend's nearby quarry. Sharply modern in contrast, conical, the rain washed over it causing it to bleed in green streaks, blending it with the antique headstones. Under the soil, Nicky's ashes rested atop Betty's coffin, conjoining mother and son.

Robin told me that after the funeral service, mourners left the small chapel and were confronted with a dramatic dark cloud which had escaped from the Dart and hovered over the edge of the churchyard. A short, angry squall followed, hats flew, people shielded their eyes. Then a piercing beam of sunlight shone suddenly through the center of the roiling sky.

On hearing this story, T.S. Eliot's verse on the tombstone reached out to me, a performance of the modern meeting the ancient, the past embracing the present, a confirmation of Nicky's legacy:

"In the end is my beginning.
We shall not cease from exploration,
And the end of all our exploring
Will be to arrive where we started
And know the place for the first time.

Endnotes

[1]Signe Hoffos, "Portrait of the Actor as a Strolling Player, sort of . . .," *Canadian Review* (Sept./Oct., 1975): 15.

[2]I had an extended interview, carried out over two days, with Nicholas Pennell on 3-4 Aug. 1994 in Stratford, Ontario. Unless otherwise referenced, Pennell's comments are from this interview.

[3]Stephen Ouimette, personal interview, 16 Aug. 1997, Stratford, Ontario. All subsequent remarks of his are from this source or referenced "SO interview."

[4]Nicholas Pennell, interviewed on the CBC's (Canadian Broadcasting Company) *Music in my Life*, 1984. One of the audio-cassette tapes in Pennell's papers, this interview is subsequently referred to as "MML interview."

[5]Nicholas Pennell, interview with Joel Seguine, *Desert Island Disks*, WHOM, Ann Arbor, 2 Feb. 1993. Subsequent references will be to "DID interview."

[6]Diana Mady Kelley and Sue Martin, "Ripeness is All," *Windsor Review* (Spring, 1995): 43.

[7]MML interview.

[8]MML interview.

[9]Robin and Jenny Pennell, personal interview, 12-13 Aug. 1997 in Devon, England. All subsequent quotations are from this source or referenced "R&PJ interview."

[10]Kelley and Martin 43.

[11]R&JP interview.

[12]DID interview.

[13]Letter from Nicholas Pennell to his parents, Betty and Gerry Milton, 17 Feb. 1951, Collection of Robin and Jenny Pennell.

[14]Letter from Nicholas Pennell to his parents, Betty and Gerry Milton, 31 October 1952, Collection of Robin and Jenny Pennell.

[15]Pennell doubled Claudio with Tom Courtenay in *Much Ado About Nothing* in a showcase production at RADA at term's end.

[16]Hoffos 16.

[17]John Pettigrew and Jamie Portman, *Stratford: The First Thirty Years*, 2 vols., vol. I (Toronto: Macmillan of Canada, 1985) 185.

[18]MML interview.

[19]Sebastian Breaks, personal interview, 17 July 1998, London. All subsequent quotations of his are from this source or referenced as "SB interview."

[20]*Playback*, Special Collector's Edition, 1995: 24.

[21]Paul Kerr, "After Forsyte," *Primetime*, Spring, 1983: 7.

[22]22.*Woman*, May 14, 1969: 36.

[23]"Nicholas, of Forsyte Fame, is Feeling the Pinch," *The Independent* [Plymouth] 23 February 1969: 5.

[24]"Stoke Gabriel Man in Forsyte Saga," *Paignton News*, 26 October 1968: 3.

[25]Elizabeth Cowley, "Nick, a Ghost and Cockatoo at Tumbler's Bottom," *TV Times* 14 October 1971: 12.

[26]*TV Times*, 14 Oct. 1971, 12.

[27]*TV Times*, 14 Oct. 1971, 12.

[28]John Williamson, letter to Nicholas Pennell, 8 Jan. 1974, Collection of Roy Brown.

[29]PQ interview.

[30]Pat Galloway, personal interview, 13 Aug. 1997 in Stratford, Ontario. Subsequent comments of hers are from this interview or referenced "PG interview."

[31]Janet Wright, personal interview, 12 Aug. 1997. Subsequent comments of hers are from this interview or referenced "JW interview."

[32]From an audio-taped interview of Pennell and three other actors in the Stratford Festival Company at that time, 30 June 1977. Interviewer is not identified. Tape is located in the Stratford Festival Archives.

[33]PQ interview.

[34]Nicholas Pennell, audio-taped interview with Rachel Urist, 1981 [no precise date or further identification available], Stratford Festival Archives. This is subsesquently referenced as "RU interview."

[35]Michael Leech, *The Stage and Television Today* 12 August 1982: 37.

[36]Nicholas Pennell, letter to Robin and Jenny Pennell, 14 July 1973, Collection of Robin and Jenny Pennell.

[37]John Pettigrew and Jamie Portman, *Stratford: The First Thirty Years*, vol. II (Toronto: Macmillan of Canada, 1985) 163.

[38]Leech 37.

[39]Leech 37.

[40]RU interview.

[41]RU interview.

[42]These comments were part of John Hirsch's letter in the Festival's souvenir program for 1985, Stratford Festival Archives.

[43]The group was referred to by this nickname among the actors as well as in the local press.

[44]For more detail, see Chapter 25, "The Crisis," in Pettigrew and Portman's *Stratford: The First Thirty Years*, vol. II, pp. 187-227.

[45]Nicholas Pennell, interview with Ivor Novello, CBC, 17 June 1981. Subsequent references are to the "IN interview."

[46]IN interview.

[47]IN interview.

[48]MML interview.

[49]IN interview.

[50]Nicholas Pennell, interviewed on *Inside Entertainment* [interviewer not identified], CKCO, Kitchener, 1991 [precise date not available}. Subsequent references will be to IN interview.

[51]IN interview.

[52]PQ interview.

[53]See letter from Nicholas Pennell to John Lawson, 8 January 1981, drafted shortly after the internal revolt. See also Actors' Committee memorandum listing demands sent to John Hirsch on 16 October 1982. Both are in Nicholas Pennell Papers, Stratford Festival Archives.

[54]PQ interview.

[55]Nicholas Pennell, interviewed on *Stereo Morning* [interviewer and station not named] 28 May 1979. Subsequent references are to "SM interview."

[56]PQ interview.

[57]MML interview.

[58]SM interview.

[59]John Broome, personal interview, 14 Aug. 1997, Stratford, Ontario. Subsequent references are to "JB interview."

[60]MML interview.

[61]Nicholas Pennell, interview on audiotape by Susan Smith, 1984 [no further identification available], Stratford Festival Archives, subsequently referenced as "SS interview."

[62]David Nicolette, "Two Decades at Stratford Give Actor a Keen View of the Festival," *Grand Rapids Press*, 13 June 1992: F2.

[63]Hoffos 16.

[64]PQ interview.

[65]Marti Maraden was interviewed by Lisa Brant in May, 1998. Unless otherwise referenced, her comments are from this interview, hereafter referred to as "MM interview."

[66]MM interview.

[67]Robert I. Schneideman, Professor of Dramatic Production at Northwestern University, critique of the Festival players Marti Maraden and Nicholas Pennell, departmental report, 12 Feb. 1979, Nicholas Pennell Papers, Stratford Festival Archives.

[68]William Mootz, "Show Charms with Literature, Gossip," *Courier Journal* (Louisville, Ky.) 6 Dec. 1977. [Item from Stratford Archives clippings file, no page number provided.]

[69]*Q's Reviews*, radio reviews of arts, CHQM, Vancouver, Can., 22 Nov. 1977, press release, Stratford Festival Archives.

[70]David Nicolette, "Two Decades at Stratford Give Actor a Keen View of the Festival," *Grand Rapids Press*, 13 June 1993: F2.

[71]Phillips is quoted from Pettigrew and Portman, II, 53.

[72]SS interview.

[73]Nicholas Rudall was interviewed in Chicago on 19 Aug. 1997. All subsequent comments of his are from this interview or referenced as "NR interview."

[74]Michael Halberstam was interviewed by telephone on 11 Aug. 1997. All subsequent comments of his are from this conversation or referenced "MH interview."

[75]MML interview.

[76]SS interview.

[77]"You Create the Role Out of Yourself," *Stratford Beacon Herald* 27 Aug. 1983 [Clipping from Burrelle's, no page number given], Stratford Festival Archives].

[78]Pettigrew and Portman, II, 66.

[79]Pettigrew and Portman, II, 78.

[80]Kelley and Martin 35.

[81]Kelley and Martin 40.

[82]MML interview.

[83]Pettigrew and Portman, II, 45.

[84]MML interview.

[85]Pettigrew and Portman, II, 64.

[86]PQ interview.

[87]I carried out a telephone interview with Patsy Rodenburg on 16 November 1999. Subsequent comments by her are from this interview or referenced "PR interview."

[88]DID interview.

[89]NR interview.

[90]SS interview.

[91]From an audio-taped interview of Pennell and three other actors in the Stratford Festival Company at that time, 30 June 1977. Interviewer is not identified. Tape is located in the Stratford Festival Archives.

[92]SS interview.

[93]PQ interview.

[94]SS interview.

[95]RU interview.

[96]IN interview.

[97]Lawrence Devine, "Pennell in his Time Played Many Parts," *Detroit FreePress* 12 March 1995: 5G.

[98]MML interview.

[99]Doug Bale, "Hamlet given two interpretations," *London Evening Free Press* (London, Ontario, Canada) 8 March 1976. Please note that the newspaper articles quoted from regarding the performances of the dual *Hamlet* were taken from the newspaper clipping files in the Stratford Archives, which offer no page numbers other than that of the file.

[100]John Fraser, "The boy Hamlet back in the role that brought him so much heartache," *Toronto Globe and Mail* (Toronto, Ontario, Canada) 21 February 1976.

[101]*Toronto Globe and Mail*, 21 February 1976.

[102]*Toronto Globe and Mail*, 21 February 1976.

[103]Myron Galloway, "A Tale of Two Hamlets," *Montreal Star* (Montreal, Quebec, Canada) 6 March 1976.

[104]William Glover, "One Play, 2 Actors, 2 Hamlets," *The San Diego Union* (San Diego, California) 23 May 1976. This story was filed by Associated Press Drama Writer Glover in 24 American newspapers, from Atlanta to Ann Arbor, during the week of 23 May-13 June 1976.

[105]*Montreal Star*, 6 March 1976.

[106]*Montreal Star*, 6 March 1976.

[107]James Nelson, "Skill symbolizes actors' differences," *Brantford Expositor* (Brantford, Ontario, Canada) 21 February 1976.

[108]*London Evening Free Press*, 8 March 1976.

[109]*London Evening Free Press*, 8 March 1976

[110]John Fraser, "On the road with Hamlet(s): not hamstrung but still hampered," *Toronto Globe and Mail* (Toronto, Ontario, Canada), 20 March 1976.

[111]Gina Mallet, "Stratford's young Hamlets worthy contenders both, *Toronto Star* (Toronto, Ontario, Canada) 19 August 1976.

[112]Pamela Cornell, "Ophelia with two Hamlets—'I simply react,'" *Ottawa Citizen* (Ottawa, Ontario, Canada) 6 March 1976.

[113]From an article in the *Hamilton Spectator* (Hamilton, Ontario, Canada) dated 12 June 1976, "... played miserably in both versions by Michael Liscinsky." From the *Ingersoll Times* (Ingersoll, Ontario, Canada) 16 June 1976, "Mr. Liscinsky just does not fit the part." There were several more no-holds-barred critiques of Claudius' character.

[114]"New Plays," *Lady* (2 February 1981) 24.

[115]"Virginia," *Financial Times*, 30 January 1981.

[116]"Virginia," *The Guardian*, 30 January 1981.

[117]"Maggie Smith's 'Virginia,'" *Daily Telegraph*, 31 January 1981.

[118]"Saved by Smith," *The Sunday Telegraph*, 21 February 1982, 14.

[119]PQ interview.

[120]Nicholas Pennell, personal interview, 3-4 Aug., 1994

[121]RM interview.

[122]SO interview.

[123]PQ interview.

[124]Kelley and Martin, 38

[125]Nigel Nicholson, letter to Nicholas Pennell, 23 Feb. 1981, Nicholas Pennell Papers, Stratford Festival Archives.

[126]Nicholas Pennell, personal interview, 16 Aug. 1994.

[127]SS interview

[128]Kelley and Martin 36-37.

[129]Nicholas Pennell, personal interview, 16 Aug. 1994.

[130]Kelley and Martin 36-37.

[131]NR interview.

[132]SO interview.

[133]David William, letter to Nicholas Pennell, 19 Sept. 1989, Nicholas Pennell Papers, Stratford Festival Archives.

[134]Robin Phillips, letter to Nicholas Pennell, undated, Nicholas Pennell papers, Stratford Festival Archives.

[135]JB interview.

[136]Kelley and Martin 40.

[137]Kelley and Martin 42

[138]PG interview.

[139]I interviewed David New in Chicago on 26 Nov. 1997. Subsequent comments of his are from that interview or referenced "DN interview."

[140]NR interview.

[141]DN interview.

[142]Denis Johnston, letter to Nicholas Pennell, 18 Feb. 1995, Nicholas Pennell Papers, Stratford Festival Archives.

[143]Bennett Solway, letter to Nicholas Pennell, 2 Dec. 1995, Nicholas Pennell Papers, Stratford Festival Archives.

[144]L.D. Jacobs, letter to Nicholas Pennell, 16 Feb. 1995, Nicholas Pennell Papers, Stratford Festival Archives.

[145]Veronica Tennant, letter to Nicholas Pennell, 15 Feb. 1995, Nicholas Pennell, Papers, Stratford Festival Archives.

[146]Desmond Heeley, letter to Nicholas Pennell, 13 Feb. 1995, Nicholas Pennell Papers, Stratford Festival Archives.

[147]Pat Galloway, letter to Nicholas Pennell, 18 Feb. 1995, Nicholas Pennell Papers, Stratford Festival Archives.

[148]Nicholas Pennell, to Stratford Festival Company, 19 Feb. 1995, Nicholas Pennell Papers, Stratford Festival Archives.

[149]"In Memoriam," *The Shakespeare Newsletter* 224, (Spring 1995): 12+.

[150]RM interview.

[151]Marian Stoddard, letter to Nicholas Pennell, 16 Feb. 1995, Nicholas Pennell papers, Stratford Festival Archives.

[152]Richard Monette, postcard to Nicholas Pennell, 6 June 1978, Nicholas Pennell Papers, Stratford Festival Archives.

[153]RM interview.

[154]Patsy Rodenburg, telephone interview, 16 November 1999.

[155]I interviewed Roy Brown in Stratford, Ontario, on 23 July 1997.

[156]From an audio-taped interview of Pennell and three other actors in the Stratford Festival Company at that time, 30 June 1977. Interviewer is not identified. Tape is located in the Stratford Festival Archives.

[157]Kelley and Martin 42.

A selective performance history of Nicholas Pennell

Nicholas Pennell had roles in more than 250 television productions, among them the BBC series *THE FORSYTE SAGA* (1966), in which he played Michael Mont. His other television appearances, prior to settling in Canada, included *THE BROTHERS KARAMAZOV, TALE OF TWO CITIES*, and *THE DOCTORS* as well as numerous dramas such as *THE VORTEX, POOR BITOS*, and *TRAPPED*.

His stage appearances in the West End in London included *A NIGHT OUT* at the Comedy Theatre and *MASTERPIECE* at the Royalty. With the Oxford Playhouse, he was in *THE ALCHEMIST* and played opposite Judi Dench in Anouilh's *ROMEO AND JEANNETTE*. He acted with the Bristol Old Vic in *THE THREE SISTERS* and *AS YOU LIKE IT*. Later on, the Stratford Festival production of *VIRGINIA* toured to the Haymarket Theatre in 1981, where he played Leonard to Maggie Smith's Virginia.

In Canada, he performed in numerous film and television productions, notably as Satie in *SATIE AND SUZANNE*. He also worked at theatres in Toronto and Boston (Scrooge in *A CHRISTMAS CAROL*). He returned to Chicago often, where he played John Aubrey in *BRIEF LIVES*, Macbeth in *MACBETH*, Sassoon in *NOT ABOUT HEROES*; he was nominated for the Joseph Jefferson Award there for Henry Higgins in *PYGMALION* in 1989. During the 1970s and 1980s, he concurrently performed and directed during his residencies at the University of Michigan, acting *A VARIABLE PASSION* there, in Chicago, and other one-man shows on campuses in Canada and the U.S.

His filmography was comprised of *RASPUTIN AND THE MAD MONK* (1966); *ISADORA* (1968); *BATTLE OF BRITAIN* (1969); *ONLY WHEN I LARF* (1969); *DAVID COPPERFIELD* (1970); *FORBUSH AND THE PENGUINS* (1971).

Most of Pennell's performances, beginning in 1972 with Orlando, were carried out at the Stratford Festival in Canada. A selected list of these roles follows.

Orlando *AS YOU LIKE IT* 1972
Tebaldeo *LORENZACCIO* 1972
Charles Marlow *SHE STOOPS TO CONQUER* 1972/3
Pericles *PERICLES, PRINCE OF TYRE* 1973, 1974, 1975
Berowne *LOVE'S LABOUR'S LOST* 1974
Antipholus/Syracuse *THE COMEDY OF ERRORS* 1975
Proteus *THE TWO GENTLEMEN OF VERONA* 1975
John Worthing *THE IMPORTANCE OF BEING EARNEST*
    1975, 1976, 1979
Hamlet *HAMLET, PRINCE OF DENMARK* 1976
Ariel *THE TEMPEST* 1976
Bertram *ALL'S WELL THAT ENDS WELL* 1977
Osvald Alving *GHOSTS* 1977
Mercutio *ROMEO AND JULIET* 1977
Victor Prynne *PRIVATE LIVES* 1978
Brutus *THE TRAGEDY OF JULIUS CAESAR* 1978
King Richard II *THE TRAGEDY OF KING RICHARD II* 1979
Iago *THE TRAGEDY OF OTHELLO* 1979
Leonard *VIRGINIA* 1980, 1981
Philinte *THE MISANTHROPE* 1981
Falkland *THE RIVALS* 1981
Ephraim Smooth *WILD OATS* 1981
Cassius *THE TRAGEDY OF JULIUS CAESAR* 1982
Ford *MERRY WIVES OF WINDSOR* 1982

David Frank *A VARIABLE PASSION* 1982
Jacques *AS YOU LIKE IT* 1983, 1984
Macbeth *THE TRAGEDY OF MACBETH* 1983
Boyet *LOVE'S LABOUR'S LOST* 1983
Holofernes *LOVE'S LABOUR'S LOST* 1984
Oberon/Theseus *A MIDSUMMER NIGHT'S DREAM* 1984
Cleante *TARTUFFE* 1984, 1985
Fool *THE TRAGEDY OF KING LEAR* 1985
Angelo *MEASURE FOR MEASURE* 1985
Malvolio *TWELFTH NIGHT* 1985
Camillo *THE WINTER'S TALE* 1986
Siegfried Sassoon *NOT ABOUT HEROES* 1987, 1988
Ulysses *TROILUS AND CRESSIDA* 1987
Gayev *THE CHERRY ORCHARD* 1987
Thomas Becket *MURDER IN THE CATHEDRAL* 1988
Antonio *MERCHANT OF VENICE* 1989
Titus *THE TRAGEDY OF TITUS ANDRONICUS* 1989
Loveless *THE RELAPSE* 1989
Jack *HOME* 1990
Banquo *THE TRAGEDY OF MACBETH* 1990
Julius Caesar *THE TRAGEDY OF JULIUS CAESAR* 1990
Peter Stockman *ENEMY OF THE PEOPLE*1991
Magnus Eisengrim *WORLD OF WONDERS* 1992
Lucio *MEASURE FOR MEASURE* 1992
Kadmos *THE BACCHAE* 1993
King John *THE LIFE AND DEATH OF KING JOHN* 1993

Recipient of the Tyrone Guthrie award - 1991

Printed in the United States
89410LV00002B/144/A